MULTINATIONAL CORPORATIONS
AND THE THIRD WORLD

MULTINATIONAL CORPORATIONS AND THE THIRD WORLD

SOM DEO

ASHISH PUBLISHING HOUSE
8/81, PUNJABI BAGH,
NEW DELHI-110026

Published by :
S.B. Nangia
for **Ashish Publishing House**
8/81, Punjabi Bagh,
New Delhi-110026
Tele : 500581
5410924

ISBN 81—7024—051—4

1986

Printed at :
Sheetal Printing Press
G-1, Prahlad Market, Karol Bagh,
New Delhi-110005

PREFACE

Global Corporations (commonly known as the multinational corporations) have appeared on the world scene as one of the most important economic force to be reckoned with. These have so much naturalised their names and products that some feel that nothing exist beyond these corporations and products. At the same time the impact of multinational corporations on our daily life cannot be overstated. The multinational corporations have been using offensive and defensive strategies suited to their requirements. Their size, growth and socio-economic and political dimensions have given rise to world wide criticism in all walks of life. It is feared that by 2000 A.D. the entire globe will be dominated by world's top two hundred corporations. The host developing countries will be used for captive production without regarding their developmental needs. Political interference will continue to loom large over the small nation States like that of Latin America, Africa and some Asian nations. These have become the States within States. If the multinational corporations are not controlled they will continue to disturb the resource base of the developing countries to the advantages of the former.

It is the legitimate right of every developing country playing host to these giant corporations to control them subserve the needs of development. It is with this objective the present study has been carried out.

My sincere thanks go to my colleagues in the Department who from time to time helped me in refining my disjointed thoughts on the problem. I am particularly grateful to Dr. H.C. Sharma, Shri C.R. Kothari, Associate Professors in the University Department of Economic Administration and Financial Management ; Shri H.C. Rara, Associate Professor in the University Department of Accountancy and Business Statistics and Dr. H.M. Mathur, Associate Professor and former Principal, Shri Ram College of Commerce, New Delhi for inspiring me from time to time. I am extremely grateful to my colleague and friend (Miss)

Sarita Jain who took tremendous pains in finalising the draft of the study.

I am thankful to those officials and employees who extended their co-operation in the conducting the study and wish to remain anonymous. Sincere thanks are due to Dr. G.S. Gupta, Professor of Economics and Dr. D. Tripathi, Professor of Business History at IIM, Ahmedabad for having discussed and solved various problems relating to this study. Mr. Dhule, Librarian at the IIM, Ahmedabad also deserves for my gratefulness for helping me in collecting the information by using the library.

I would be failing from my duties if I do not express my sincere thanks to Dr. Om Prakash, Senior Professor, Department of Economic Administration and Financial Management, University of Rajasthan who was the main source of guidance and inspiration for the study. He was not only a philosopher guide but a profound thinker on the subject who impressed my thinking more than often. His perception proved to be an asset to me.

Professor Clem Tisdell, Department of Economics, New Castle University, New South Wales, Australia deserves special thanks for going through the manuscript and giving his valueable suggestions. I differed from him at various points but greatly impressed by his thoughts. Some of his observations helped me in modifying and refreshing my thoughts which facilitated my effort to a very great extent. His erudition and sharp perception of the situation is, no doubt, unequivocal.

I have no words to express my gratitude towards my wife, Mrs. Santosh, who was put to lots of inconvenience during the study.

I thank Mr. O.P. Gupta for typing neatly the manuscript and Mr. Nangia of M/S Ashish Publishing House, New Delhi who brought the volume in time with such a good printing.

SOM DEO

Jaipur

CONTENTS

LIST OF TABLES

LIST OF ABBREVIATIONS

ASEAN	Association of South East Asian Nations.
ESCAP	Economic and Social Commission for Asia and the Pacific.
FDI	Foreign Direct Investment.
FCRCs	Foreign Controlled Rupee Companies.
FERA	Foreign Exchange Regulation Act.
ITT	International Telephone and Telegraph.
ILO	International Labour Office.
IDPL	Indian Drugs and Pharmaceutical Limited.
MNCs	Multinational Corporations.
MNE	Multinational Enterprise.
NECS	National Entry Control System.
OECD	Organisation for Economic Corporation and Development.
RBPs	Restrictive Business Practices.
TNC	Transnational Corporations.
UNCTAD	United Nations Conference on Trade and Development.

INTRODUCTION

A Brief Historical Background

Multinational Corporation—Concept

Legal Definition of MNCs

The Problem

Power of the MNCs

MNC : A Powerful Instrument for the Flow of Investment

Transfer of Technology and Other Economic Dimensions

Clashing with National Sovereignty

Where do the MNCs Conflict with the Host Countries

Multinational Corporations and India

Objectives of the Study

Hypotheses of the Study

Methodology

1

Introduction

A BRIEF HISTORICAL BACKGROUND

Historically transnational trading was conducted by Greek, Phoenician and Mesopotemian merchants ; but gradually Europe and the Middle East stepped into feudalism following the fall of the Roman Empire, and trade between nations became more difficult because of the wars between feudal lords and the Church's influence in prohibiting trade with the Muslim States. The commerce established by the later merchant traders of Italy can be considered forerunners of the multinational firms. The Crusades, which started in 1095, caused the city States of Genoa, Venice, Florence and Pisa to flourish since these places served as staging areas and supply depots for the Crusades. As a money economy replaced the prevailing barter economy, banks and money leading institutions developed and flourished, leading to active transnational operations. Multinationals, in the form of trading company started in 17th and 18th centuries. The Hudson Bay Co., the East India Co., the French Levant Co., are examples. Export and import houses and commercial and financial institutions prospered.

Originally all these transnational entities limited themselves to trading (like that of East India Co.) but gradually they started to govern the lines of their producers. Since they brought with them their own armies and religious missionaries, they also came to exercise control over the territories.

During the 19th century, foreign investment flowed extensively from Western Europe to the underdeveloped areas of Asia, Africa and the Americas including the USA. Britain was a great

capital exporter, followed by France, the Netherlands and
Germany ; however, most of this capital flow was in the form of
direct investment inside the imperial boundaries. Consequently
British firms made extensive investments in India, Canada,
Australia and S. Africa ; French Co. in Indochina, Algeria and
other overseas colonies, and Dutch capital flowed to the East
Indies, and, in lesser degrees to the West Indies. The colonial
powers had captive markets and raw material resources in their
colonies.

During the earlier years of 20th century, substantial multinational corporate investment went into mining and petroleum
industries ; large oil Co. such as British Petroleum and Standard
Oil were the first multinationals in this area ; and other mineral
corporations, such as Anaconda Copper and International Nickel,
moved in quickly. Multinational corporate investment got a boost
following world war I, when protectionist policies of nations
States spurred firms to jump the trade barriers raised by the
nation States by replacing exports with foreign production.
Gradually manufacturing and merchandising multinationals such
as Unilever/Lever Brothers, Nestle, Coca Cola, International
Harvester, Singer, Philips NV, Woolworth, Imperial Chemical
Industries, Ford Motors, Texas Instruments, etc., and various
German drugs and chemical firms, began operating on a world
wide scale. American corporate multinational enterprises investment moved extensively to Canada, Europe and South America
and to the Middle East for oil.

The multinational enterprise is not new. What is relatively
new, however, is the magnitude of the multinational enterprise
and the extent to which its international operations have become
interwoven from technical, production, managerial, marketing,
financial, accounting and personnel points of view. Economic
activities throughout the world, spurred by technological ad-
vances, have given impetus to the structures of companies whose
large scale operations cross national and even political boundaries
of nation—States, and thus considered a threat to the autonomy
of these States. The modern multinational corporation, accord-
ingly, is based on more than just trading. It tries to optimise its
international production and marketing, often doing so by the use

of trade marks and patents. This is one of the most significant structural changes in the history of international economic institutions and economic order.

MULTINATIONAL CORPORATIONS : CONCEPT

One common concept, running through all the definitions, is the significant role played by these corporations in the internationalisation of the world economy. Non-declaration of information by these corporations is regarded as a sacred right, and secrecy shrouds their activities. It was in this context that Raymond Vernon was forced to delimit his study to foreign companies controlling a large cluster of corporations of various nationalities with sales of 100 billion dollars or more, and he termed such a group as a Multinational Enterprise.[1] Largely influenced by this approach, the United Nations document on 'Multinational Corporations in World Development' has also taken the size and concentration as the basic criteria for identification of Multinational Corporations, and has listed 650 industrial corporations with sales exceeding 300 million dollars in each case.[2] Like Raymond Vernon, Dunning also avoids the expression 'corporation' possibly because of the legal implications of the word 'corporation' which is a distinct and separate juristic person, and introduces the concept of International Enterprise. He classifies them into four categories, *viz.*, Multinational Producing Enterprise (MPE), Multinational Trading Enterprise (MTE), Multinational Owned Enterprise (MOE) and Multinational Controlled Enterprise (MCE).[3] The government of Canada has fixed a minimum number of four or five countries across which a single business enterprise straddles, as the basic criterion for defining a Multinational Enterprise.[4] According to the Business International, a firm becomes multinational when foreign operations account for at least 35 per cent of its total sales and profits.[5]

---

1. Vernon, Raymond, 'Sovereignty at Bay : The Multinational Spread of US Enterprises', New York, Basic Books, 1971, p. 4.
2. No. 7 (b), pp. 6 and 127.
3. Dunning, John H, 'The Multinational Enterprise—The Background, Chapter I, Allen and Unwin, London, 1971.
4. See discussion on Foreign Direct Investment in Canada, Ottawa, 1972, p. 51. Report Popularly known as Grey Report.
5. Business International, Organising for Its World Wide Operations, New York, 1965, p. 15.

MacDonald and Parker consider a firm to be multinational if 20 per cent of its assets are overseas.[6]

The US Tariff Commission Report points out that an enterprise can qualify itself a Multinational if it has at least 25 per cent participation in the share of the foreign enterprise. But the US department of Commerce data are based on equity holding as low as 10 per cent.[7]

David E. Lilienthal draws wider parameter when he defines multinational corporations as corporations which have their home in one country but operate and live under the laws and customs of other countries as well.[8]

Perlmutter's definition, frequently referred to in treaties on Transnational Corporations, classifies the corporations on the basis of geographic orientation of activities. The three suggested classifications are : ethno-centric (Home country oriented), polycentric (host country oriented) and geo-centric (world oriented).[9] This definition suffers from an over-simplification because the orientation test is not capable of application in the absence of data regarding the interests involved in corporate decision-making. In this study various terms of Multinational Enterprise, Transnational Corporation, Multinational owned Enterprise and Multinational Controlled Enterprise have been used interchangeably with the Multinational Corporation (MNC).

LEGAL DEFINITION OF THE MNCs

The Commission on Transnational Corporations has been wrestling with the question of identifying the corporation or organisation to be called as Multinational Corporation. But it is still unable to arrive at a commonly acceptable definition.[10] This,

---

6. International Enterprise ; Creating a Strategy for International Growth, 1962, pp. 17-19.
7. US Tariff Commission, 'Report on Impact of Multinational Firms', TC Publications, Washington, D.C. Feb. 1973, p. 81.
8. Lilienthal, David E,. The Multinational, Corporations : Development and Resources Corporation, New York, 1960, p. 119.
9. Perlmutter, H.V., 'The Tortous Evolution of the MNCs,' Columbia Law Journal of World Business, Vol. 4, 1969.
10. UN Doc. E/C. 10/38 of 10 March, 1978, 'Transnational Corporations in World Development : A Re-examination,' Annexure I. p. 158.

of course, has not deterred the attempts to seek the basis for the purpose of such identification to be covered by a code of conduct or by national regulations or international agreements. Move in this direction has been made by Columbia and India by attempting a legislative definition of multinational corporations. In Columbia, the expression, Multinational Enterprise is defined as a "sub-regional multinational corporation, comprising of a company established in one country with participation of at least two member countries each holding at least 15 per cent of capital and a maximum 40 per cent participation : the majority sub-regional holding may be reflected in the technical, financial, administrative and commercial management of the enterprise."[11]

In India, a specific definition of MNC as such appears in Foreign Contribution Regulation Act, 1973. For the purpose of this Act a corporation incorporated in a foreign country or territory shall be deemed to be a multinational corporation, if such corporation :

(*a*) is a subsidiary or a branch or has place of business in two or more countries or territories ;

(*b*) carries on business or otherwise operations in two or more countries or territories ;

Of the two definitions, the Indian definition is wider in its reach and goes farther than even the definition given by the Group of Eminent Persons, which said :

Multinational Corporations or Enterprises which own or control production or service facilities outside the countries in which they are based. Such enterprises are not always incorporated or private. They can also be co-operative or State owned entities.[12]

THE PROBLEM

The rise of multinational corporations has been the most remarkable phenomena of the post war period though having their

---

11. UN Doc. ST/CTC/6, 'National Legislation and Regulations relating to the Transnational Corporations," Table D. 2, pp. 202-5. The definition appears to relate to corporations within the Andean Group under the Agreement of Cartagena, 1969.
12. UN Doc. E/5500/Rev. 1 : ST/ESA/6, 'The Impact of the Multinational Corporation on Development and International Relations', p. 25.

centuries old roots in the global economic system with the dawn of industrial revolution. They command production and distribution network in more than one country and having wide ramifications. Their operations cover many countries and multiple product lines, which are growing at spectacular rates. Multinational corporations derive strength from their vast resource base of capital, sophisticated technology and their trade names. If their growth continues with the same rate as they did during 1970-80, by the end of this century these will contribute about one half of the world gross product. Multinational corporations have traversed through a long process of growth. Accelerating concentration of industry and banking with multinationalisation of their operations are the hallmarks of this unabated process of growth.

To streamline the growth the multinational corporations have evolved a well integrated organisational system through inter-corporate and inter-country stock holding. In order to expand their business in foreign countries they provide financial support to political parties and thereby exercise influence on government where they work. Thus they have acquired not only economic implications but political overtones also. In this process they are also provided with support, directly or indirectly, from the parent country's government through arming, financing and politically supporting the client regimes throughout the third world to repress their own people, and in some cases, to act in addition to as sub-imperialist gendarmes in their respective geographical regimes. The multinational corporate system affects the world society in several ways. It influences the society's major economic decisions, namely, what to produce, how to produce (which technology to use). These decisions determine the use of world's resources and distribution of world's production and thereby the current and future control of the global economic power.

POWER OF THE MULTINATIONAL CORPORATIONS

The spectacular growth, proliferation and influences of the MNCs on the international economy is revealed by the fact that in the early seventies, ten thousand such entities with 30 thousand subsidiaries were operating around the world.[13] By the end of this

---

13. UN informe Mundial Economico, 1981-82.

decade, estimates made by the UN Centre on Transnational Corporations put the figure at 11 thousand corporations with 82 thousand subsidiaries abroad.

The proliferation of overseas subsidiaries of the MNCs have gone hand in hand with spectacular growth of direct capital investment. In 1971 cumulative direct investment abroad amounted to $ 158 billion, by 1975 this figure was $ 259 billion and, according to recent estimates, the figure was $ 450 billion in 1980.[14] These figures assume an average growth rate of more than 12 per cent during the decade, a growth rate even larger than that of the developed capitalist economies taken as a whole during the same period.

Table 1.1
World's Largest MNCs Ranked by Sales (Year 1983)

Rank	Company	Head Qrt.	Sales ($ '000)
1	2	3	4
1.	Exxon	New York	88,561,134
2.	Royal Dutch Shell	The Hague/London	80,550,885
3.	Gen. Motors	Detroit	74,581,600
4.	Mobil	New York	54,607,000
5.	British Petroleum	London	49,194,886
6.	Ford Motor	Dearborn, Minch.	44,454,600
7.	IBM	Armonk, N.Y.	40,180,000
8.	Texaco	Harrison N.Y.	40,068,000
9.	EI du pont	Wilmington, Del.	35,378,000
10.	Standard Oil (Ind.)	Chicago	27,635,000
11.	Standard Oil (Cal.)	San Francisco	25,342,000
12.	General Electric	Fairfield, Conn.	26,797,000
13.	Gulf Oil	Pittsburgh	26,581,000
14.	Atlantic Richfield	Los Angeles	25,147,036
15.	ENI	Rome	25,022,358
16.	IRI	Rome	24,518,447
17.	Unilever	London/Rotterdam	20,291,583
18.	Toyota Motor	Toyota, Japan	19,741,094
19.	Shell Oil	Houston	19,678,000
20.	Occidental Petr.	Los Angeles	19,115,700
21.	Francaise des Petr.	Paris	18,350,186
22.	Elf-Aquitaine	Paris	18,188,156
23.	US Steel	Pittsburgh	16,869,000
24.	Matsushita Elect.	Osaka	16,719,440
25.	Petrobras	Rio de Janeiro	16,258,011

(Contd.)

14. OECD, Economic Outlook, No. 32, Dec. 1982.

Table 1.1 *(Contd.)*

1	2	3	4
26.	Philips Gloeilampen-fabrieken	Eindhoven (Neth.)	16,176,941
27.	Pemex	Mexico City	16,140,013
28.	Hitachi	Tokyo	15,804,301
29.	Siemens	Munich	15,724,273
30.	Nissan Motor	Yokohama	15,697,733
31.	Volkswagenwerk	Wolfsburg	15,697,352
32.	Daimler-Benz	Stuttgart	15,660,437
33.	Phillips Petroleum	Bartlesville, Okla	15,249,000
34.	Sun	Radnor, Pa	14,730,000
35.	United Technologies	Hartford	14,669,265
36.	Bayer	Leverkusen (Ger.)	14,615,594
37.	Hoechst	Frankfurt	14,558,235
38.	Renault	Paris	14,467,765
39.	Fiat	Turin (Italy)	14,466,548
40.	Tenneco	Houston	14,353,000
41.	ITT	New York	14,155,408
42.	Nestle	Vevey (Switz.)	13,303,618
43.	BASF	Ludwigshafen on Rhine	13,250,424
44.	Chrysler	Highland Park, Mich.	13,240,399
45.	Volvo	Goteberg (Swed.)	12,963,008
46.	Imperial Chemical Industries	London	12,750,075
47.	Proctor & Gamble	Cincinnati, Ohio	12,452,000
48.	BAT Industries	London	12,083,087
49.	R.J. Reynolds Industries	Winston-Salem, NC	11,957,000
50	Mitsubishi Heavy Industries	Tokyo	11,916,254
		Total	1,211,907,851

Source : Fortune, August 20, 1984, p. 201.

As a consequence, the control of technology by the world's top 200 corporations, of finance by the top 20 banks, and of the instruments of developing and disseminating information and ideology by the largest advertising agencies, the top television networks and newspaper chain have become pervasive in the so-called 'free world.' In the present day world economy MNCs have acquired such a dominating position that they have undermined the traditional role of national and international institutions and free market in determining the allocation of resources. These enterprises have grown bigger than even the nation States, their operations have become more powerful than national policies and their organisational network has made the existing institutional framework ineffective and obsolete.

MNCs : A POWERFUL INSTRUMENT FOR THE FLOW OF INVESTMENT

Heavy investments have been made by developed countries (especially by the USA) in developing world. But the resources repatriated from the developing countries to the developed world (either in terms of profit, royalty or otherwise) have been much higher. As can be noted from the Table 1.2, for every new dollar invested in all the underdeveloped countries during the period, MNCs repatriated approximately $2.2 to their home countries. In the specific case of US MNCs, on which more information is available, during 1970-79 they invested $11,446 million and repatriated profits amounting to $ 48,663 million which means no less than a $4.25 return from the third world for every new dollar invested. If 1980 were included the figure would be even higher. And if the year 1984 is also taken into account the figure would be really staggering.

Table 1.2

Foreign Direct Investment (FDI) Flow to Underdeveloped Countries and Profits on Direct Investment Repatriated to Investor Countries

Under-developed Countries	*(Accrued Sums 1970-80)* Net flow of FDI in underdeveloped countries	*(in millions of $)* Profits on direct investment repatriated to investor countries
Total of underdeveloped Countries	62,615	1,39,703
Latin America	33,437	38,642
Africa	10,341	23,916
Middle East	57 (*)	48,619
Southern & S.E. Asia	18,048	27,260
Oceania	732	1,266

Source : Based on UNCTAD, Handbook on International Trade and Development Statistics, Supplement 1981, pp. 264-265.

(*) : This low figure is due to disinvestment during that period.

One more Table (Table 1.3) shows the degree of exploitation the US MNCs are inflicting on underdeveloped countries.

Table 1.3
USA 1970-1980
Net Flow of Direct Investment, Total Profits Repatriated and Reinvested, by Selective Regions

(million $)

Investment Recipients Areas	(A)	(B)	(C)	(D)	(E)	(F)
All Areas	44,009	1,22,705	97,283	2,19,988	56	18.4
Developed Countries	35,399	63,482	71,850	1,35,332	47	16.6
Underdeveloped Countries	7,922	55,988	23,338	79,326	71	24.1
others	618	3,235	2,095	5,330	61	15.1

Source : Survey of Current Business, August 1980 and 1981.

Notes : (A) Net flow of direct investments

(B) Profits repatriated to the USA

(C) Re-invested profits

(D) Total profits

(E) Percentage of total profits repatriated to the USA

(F) Profit rates on cumulative investments in 1981 (%).

Table 1.3 shows that under-developed countries receive only 18 per cent of the total flow of direct investments as compared to 80 per cent in the developed countries. Yet, under-developed countries contributed 36 per cent of the total world profits earned by the US MNCs, accounting for 46 per cent of all profits repatriated to the USA. This means that 71 per cent of the profits made in the under-developed countries were repatriated and only the remainder were re-invested in the host countries. On the other hand, only 47 per cent of the profits earned in the developed capitalist world was repatriated. It must be added that the profit rate declared by US multinationals in the underdeveloped countries was 24.1 per cent ; this easily surpasses both the rates attained in the developed countries (16.6 per cent) and the world rate (18.4 per cent).

Various conclusions can be drawn from these figures. Firstly, as a result of a clear cut profit repatriation strategy by the US corporations, the under-developed countries are the greatest contributors to that country's balance of payment. Secondly, as a consequence of the above, the US MNCs increase their hold and expand. Thirdly, high profit rates in under-developed countries lead to continuous decapitalisation of the under-developed world.

TRANSFER OF TECHNOLOGY AND OTHER ECONOMIC DIMENSIONS

Most of the technology supplied by the MNCs are capital-intensive, import oriented and obsolete. A lure of sophisticated technology has been completely unsuitable to needs of the developing world. Once the developing country gets foreign technology from the MNCs there happens to be a vicious circle of technology and resulting into 'technological trap.' It is a well known fact that almost 80 per cent of technology is marketed by the MNCs to their subsidiaries as a property of the latter and not of the developing countries.

Role of MNCs in acting as agent for technology, product and innovation might be limited. This is because the MNC generally undertakes important R and D activities in the home country and only occasionally in the host country ; this might also apply to technology innovation, though perhaps to a lesser extent. Attempts will be made in the present study to examine whether foreign firms and local firms carry out significantly different amounts of R and D activities and the training of workers, whether foreign firms do act as an important agent for technology transfer and whether the presence of foreign firms does increase the rate of technical progress in that country (A detailed analysis is made in Chapter 3 with supporting cases in India and other developing countries playing host to the multinational corporations).

At the same time, the MNCs' operations in the host country have other economic dimensions also. There are, use of transfer pricing, restrictive business practices and their consequent impact on economy as a whole in general and on allocation of resources and balance of payment in particular (discussed in detail in Chapters 4 and 5).

CLASHING WITH THE NATIONAL SOVEREIGNTY

The multinational corporations do not bother much about the legislation of the countries where they operate, *e.g.*, in the field of investments, their tax, trade, labour and price policies. They also intervene directly or indirectly in the internal affairs of the host country. MNCs refuse to accept, covertly or overtly, the exclusive jurisdiction of the domestic laws of the host country as regards to compensation in case of nationalisation.

Then there is a question of regulating the activities of MNCs. Whether they should be regulated by persuasion or code of conduct or by legislative measures. These aspects have been debated for quite a long time and the recommendations of the Group of Eminent Persons have given further momentum to this debate. The new international economic order is also open to question without giving a thought to the problem of MNCs *vis-a-vis* the world economic system. But at the same time the world economy appears as much disintegrated as it is integrated today.

WHERE DO THE MNCs CONFLICT WITH THE HOST COUNTRIES

Conflict between the MNCs and the host government may derive from four sources : from the fact that it is 'private' and hence may clash with the social and national goals ; that it is 'large' and oligopolistic and hence possesses market and bargaining power which may be used against the interest of the host country; that it is 'foreign' and hence may be serving the national interest of a foreign nation ; and that it is 'western' and hence may transfer inappropriate know-how, technology or management practices, or products designed with characteristics not suitable in less developed countries.

A schematic presentation will help us understand where and how do the MNCs clash with the interests, and consequently with sovereignty, of the host countries, especially of the host developing countries.

Objective of the Multinational Corporation	Objective of the Host Countries
1. What, where and with what inputs to produce to maximise profits.	What and with what inputs to produce within the country to maximise growth and social justice.
2. Where and on what scale R and D to be undertaken to serve the above objective.	Within the country with permissible resources R and D to be undertaken to serve the objective.
3. The inter-subsidiary movements of goods and services and their pricing.	The inter-regional movements of goods and services at national price levels.
4. To achieve higher productivity.	To achieve higher employment.
5. To strengthen the MNC	To strengthen national economy.
6. Human resource development for the exploitation of natural resources.	Exploitation of natural resources for human resource development.
7. To achieve international integration, *i.e.*, domination.	To achieve national self-sufficiency.
8. To maximise sale through unbalanced growth.	To maximise balanced growth.
9. To meet military needs.	To combine development with defence needs.

MULTINATIONAL CORPORATIONS AND INDIA

In India 358 branches and 128 subsidiaries of MNCs were working as at the end of 1978-79.[16] This number was 540 and 188 respectively in 1973-74. Despite the decline in number total assets of both the branches and subsidiaries recorded substantial increase during 1973-74 and 1978-79. As per the data available the total assets of 434 branches was Rs. 1,790.5 crores in 1973-74 which was Rs. 2,401.35 crores for 288 branches in 1978-79. In India a wide range of products are produced by the MNCs from day to day consumer goods (like toothpaste, cigarettes, etc.) to the most sophisticated commodities (like machinery, pharmaceuticals, etc.). Out of 358 branches 85 were engaged in Agriculture and allied activities, 7 in mining and quarrying, 47 in processing and manu-

---

16. Company News and Notes, Vol. XVIII, June 1980, No. 6, p. 1.

facturing, 68 in commerce trade and finance, 58 in community and business services. An important trend has been noted with regards to the increasing number of liaison offices of MNCs. This number in 1973-74 was only 13 which went up to 28 in 1978-79.

In the same manner the number of subsidiaries has declined from 188 in 1973-74 to 125 in 1978-79 but assets have increased from Rs. 1,363.7 crores to Rs. 1,706.6 crores respectively. Highest number of subsidiaries are working in processing and manufacturing (82) followed by commerce trade and finance (18) and Agriculture and allied activities (13).

Table 1.4

Assets of Branches and Subsidiaries of MNCs in India

(Rs. in crores)

Year	Branches		Subsidiaries	
	No.	Assets	No.	Assets
1973-74	540	1,790.4 (434)	188	1,363.7
1974-75	510	2,129.8 (424)	183	1,534.6
1975-76	481	2,084.4 (393)	171	1,626.2
1976-77	482	2,178.2 (396)	161	1,649.6
1977-78	473	2,393.4 (384)	146	1,741.6
1978-79	358	2,401.4 (288)	125	1,706.6

Source : Company News and Notes, Vol. XVIII, June 1980, No. 6.

Notes : (1) figures in brackets indicate the number of branches to which the assets relate.

(2) Assets shown in Table for the years 1973-74 to 1978-79 include assets for earlier years in case of branches/subsidiaries whose balance sheets for the respective years were not available.

Some Foreign Companies in India

Dominant Foreign Companies	Product	Percentage of total distribution	Status
1	2	3	4
Liptons & Brooke Bond	Tea	85	Retail distribution
	Coffee		
Massy Ferguson and International Harvester	Rubber	33	
	Agricultural Machinery	60	Dominant
ICI, CIBA and Bayers	Insecticides and Pesticides		Dominant
Andrew Yule group, McNeil Barry, Turner Morrison, Shaw Wallace	Coal Mining		Dominant
A-V-B Limited and Mc-Nally Bird Engineering	Mining Machinery		
Hindustan Lever	Food	33	
Parry & Co. and Cadbury Fry	Toffee		Dominant
Britania Biscuit Co. and Huntley Palmer	Biscuits		Dominant
Indian Yeast Co. (Shaw Wallace)	Yeast		Monopoly
Hindustan Lever, Glaxo Laboratories and Horlicks	Milk products		Dominant
Nestles Co.	Condensed milk		Monopoly
Larson and Toubro	Dairy Machinery	50	
Indian Tobacco (UK), Vazir Sultan (British American Tobacco Co.)	Cigarettes		Dominant
Molins of India	Cigarettes Machinery		Monopoly
Tribeni Tissues Pvt. Ltd.	Cigarette Paper		Monopoly
Buckingham & Carnatic, Finlay and Madura Mills	Cotton Textiles		
Issac Holdens	Wool tops	33	
Lagan Jute Machinery Co.	Jute Machi-		

(Contd.)

1	2	3	4
and Low and Bonar Ltd.	nery		Dominant
Alkali and Chemical Corporation of India (ICI subsidiary).	Terelyne		Monopoly
Bata	Footwear	99.6	
Tin Plate Co. of India	Tin Plate	90.0	
Indian Aluminium Co. (USA), HINDALCO (Kaiser of USA)	Aluminium		Dominant
Venesta Foils Ltd.	Aluminium foil		Dominant
Acro India Ltd.	Steel framework and scaffolding		Largest
Indian Tube Co. and Tube products of India Ltd.	Steel tubes		Dominant
Tube Investment Cycles and San-Raleigh Industries of India Limited	Bicycles		Dominant
Dunlop	Cycle rims, cycle tyres, & tubes		Dominant
Ashok Leyland, Premier Automobiles	Motor Vehicles		Dominant
Dunlop, Firestone, Goodyear and Ceat	Motor tubes tyres		
Associated Battery Makers and Chloride and Excide Battery Ltd.	Motor vehicles batteries		Monopoly
Motor Industries (Robert Bosch)	Fuel Injections		Dominant
Lucas, Simmons Motor and Electronics Corporation and Robert Bosch, Dunlop, GKW	Electric Components		Dominant
Napco Bevel Gear of India	Gear		Dominant
Enfield and Escorts	Motor Cycles		
AEI, Crompton Parkinson, GEC, British India Electric Construction, Greaves Cotton, Heckbridge, Hewittie and Easum	Transformers (Electric)		

(*Contd.*)

1	2	3	4
Indian Cables Co. Henley Cables, AEI Krupps	Electric Cables		
Olivetti and Co.	Teleprinting Equipment		Monopoly
Philips, Hind Lamp manufacturers, Electric Lamp manufactures, Osler Electric Lamp manufacturing Co.	Electric lamp		Dominant
Philips, Murphy, GEC, Gramophone Co., Marconi Phone Co.	Radio Receivers		
Remington Rand	Typewriters		Dominant
Indian Explosives	Blasting explosives		Monopoly
NOCIL, Union Carbide Polyolifins, Polychem	Petro-chemical		Dominant
Sandoz products, Suhrid Geigy Trading Ltd.	Optical Bleaching agents		Dominant
Merck Sharpe Dohme, Parke Davis & Co., Geoffery Manners, Hoechst, CIBA, Cynamide, Pfizer, Glaxo, Burroughs Wellcome, Johnson and Johnson, Beecham Group Laboratories, Squibb, Roche products	Drugs and Pharmaceuticals		Monopoly in various products
ICI, Jenson & Nicholsson, British Paints (India) Ltd. Goodlass Wall, Shalimar Paints. Colour and Varnish Ltd. (Pinchin)	Paints		Dominant
Hindustan Lever, Godrej	Soap and Detergents		Dominant
WIMCO and Assam Match Co.	Matches		Dominant

OBJECTIVES AND HYPOTHESES OF THE STUDY

During the last two decades, especially in the later decade the working of the multinational corporations has sparked much of controversy. There appears to be a clear categorisation of the persons who may be called as pro-multinationals and anti-multinationals. The present study is an attempt to test empirically the hypotheses that these multinational corporations, contrary to popular belief, are constraining the host countries' resources only to the advantage of the parent firms irrespective of their nationality. The study proposes to focus empirically on three fold objectives.

(a) the objective of asserting developing countries' especially India's sovereignty over their own political and economic life ;

(b) the objective of compelling or persuading the foreign corporations to make more contribution to developing countries' (In Indian reference) growth and welfare ; and

(e) the objective of emancipating the underdeveloped countries from having to contribute 'captive production' to a vertically integrated corporate system that did not subserve host countries' interest.

The study seeks to study the following hypotheses :

(a) that the multinational corporations are responsible for disturbing the resource base and solely function to their advantage against the interest of the host countries.

(b) that the multinational corporations are interfering with the local administration by their political wranglings so as to erode the sovereignty of nation States.

(c) that the transfer of technology is nothing but farce and the host countries are being flushed with inappropriate technology.

(d) that the development of the international trade and the impact on balance of payment thereof is going against the third world in general and ‚India in ˉparticular due to the adoption of the practices by MNCs like, *Inter-alia*, transfer pricing, inter-corporate investment, restrictive business practices.

(e) that the capitalistic methods of production employed by the MNCs to produce for the 'class' and not for the 'mass' are giving rise to exploitation of consumers in particular and society at large.

METHODOLOGY

The study is based on primary and secondary source of data. The effort was made to collect the data on the basis of field surveys with the help of questionnaires and personal interviews with organisations, executives, workers, trade union leaders and also with the consumers. But non-availability of data and not-so-openness at all levels was the main predicament of the whole study. Therefore, secondary data were used in most of the analysis. These secondary data were collected from the widely acceptable authentic sources like United Nations, World Bank publications, various studies conducted by the different organisations like UNCTAD, etc. The fact of using old data somewhere is only due to the authenticity of information desired for the purpose. For, the authenticity of information was considered to be the prime consideration throughout the analyses.

The centres which were visited are mainly big cities like Ahmedabad, Bombay, Calcutta, Delhi and Madras. At the same time, those peripheral areas were also visited which were declared by the government as notified industrially backward areas and where the foreign collaborations/enterprises are making their mark to establish industrial units to reap the advantages of various concessions provided by the Central or State governments. A good amount of foreign studies were helpful in steering this study ahead. Since the personal surveys were not possible and therefore, the questionnaires were sent to some organisations. But while quoting the foreign studies the secondary data were mainly used. The biggest handicap of the study was the poor response of the persons and organisations both.

Various issues (as covered by the subsequent chapters of the study) were discussed at length and are given chapter-wise, (*viz.*, socio-political aspect of the working of multinational corporations, transfer of technology, transfer pricing and restrictive trade practices, international trade and balance of payments impacts and so on.

It is tried that conclusions and suggestions of relevant problems are given in the respective chapters, but a summary is also given in the last chapter. An effort has been made to search for regulatory mechanism suitable to the economy of developing nations at large and India in particular.

POLITICAL ECONOMY OF MULTINATIONAL CORPORATION

Introduction

Power Structure of Multinational
Corporations and the Developing
Economy

Clashing with National Sovereignty—
Some Cases in Point

Some Indian Cases in Point

Suggestions

2
Political Economy of Multinational Corporations

INTRODUCTION

Many writers have discussed the nation States *vis-a-vis* the multinational corporations. But their political overtones have been discussed by a few authors. During the last decade a discussion has been going on about two 'sovereigns' namely, the nations States of host countries and the multinational corporations. In the process of asserting their respective sovereignties there came a clash between the two. Actions of parent countries (or home countries) in such situations have added another dimension to the whole problem. Dunning is more critical of the role of multinationals then either Kindleberger or Penrose. Dunning is aware of the fundamental conflict between the multinationals and the nation States but still argues that the growth of MNCs and its continued domination of the international economy offer the best prospects for the future. Raymond Vernon finds that the MNCs, by transmitting knowledge, technology and resources efficiently across national boundaries, contribute to greater global welfare. Although troubled by some of the changes that have resulted from the growth of multinationals—particularly that many flows of goods, services, and money no longer result from arm's length transactions between national economies but from transactions between sister affiliates of multinationals—he has been most interested in the decline of national sovereignty as a consequence of the rise of the international firms.[1] Vernon has always recognised the tensions that have existed between the multinationals and the nation States, but he was optimistic that the global perspective of some of the multinationals, especially those from the United States, might enable them to transcend their narrow nationalism.[2] He, like Penrose, has suggested that a supranational authority might do much to lessen any conflict that might arise. However, the international oil crisis has led him to re-evaluate his past views.[3]

Two main events in the oil crisis impressed Vernon. The first was the inability of home governments, particularly those from the Western Europe and the United States, to affect the actions of the MNCs. As Vernon notes, the US government was particularly slow to respond to the oil crisis brought on by the quadrupling oil prices. The top levels of the administration engrossed in the problems of Watergate, remained unaware of the full implications of the crisis until nearly six months after it broke. Other governments, like the French, used the crisis to begin foreign policy initiatives that would assert their independence from the USA.[4] The Japanese Ministry for International Trade and Industry used the crisis to shore up its declining ability to control the Japanese economy.[5] Secondly, whereas Vernon has previously seen host countries as being relatively weak in comparison to the multinationals,[6] the oil crisis underscored the increased bargaining power of the OPEC nations. They had been able to improve their ability to collect and interpret the information that affected their negotiating position.

On the other hand vernon also points to the continuing, or possibly enhanced, political power of multinationals. He states that the basic problem is to find an international approach to disentangle conflicting national jurisdictions so that actions by

1. Cohen, Robert D. *et. al.*, The Multinational Corporations, Cambridge University Press, 1979, pp. 7-8.
2. Vernon, R., Sovereignty at Bay, Basic Books, New York, 1971. p. 109.
3. Vernon, R., Storm over the Multinationals : Problems and Prospects, Foreign Affairs, January 1977, pp. 243-262 and Vernon, R.. An Interpretation, in Vernon's edited, 'The Oil Crisis', W.W. Norton, New York, pp. 1-14.
4. Vernon, R., *ibid.*, pp. 2-14.
5. Tsurumi, Y., 'Japan' in Vernon's 'The Oil Crisis', *op. cit.*, pp. 113-28.
6. Vernon, Reymond, Sovereignty at Bay, Basic Books, 1971, pp. 134-35.

individual nations will not harm others, and to secure agreement among nations over what type of public actions are needed.

There are three ways in which political factors shape economic outcomes. First, the political system shapes the economic system, as the structure and operation of the international economic system is, to a great extent, determined by the structure and operation of the international political system. Second, political concerns often shape economic policy, as important economic policies are frequently dictated by overriding political interests. Third, international economic relations, in and of themselves, are political relations, as international economic interaction, like international political interaction, is a process by which State and non-State actors manage, or fail to manage, their conflicts and by which they co-operate, to achieve common goals. All international economic transactions were regulated for the purpose of State power.

People generally believe that the State, or political sphere, and the corporate, or economic sphere are independent of each other and only distantly related. For some, then determining force is the economic, political cultural and other factors are external forces that tend to distort and disrupt the economy. The conflict between the multinational corporation and the nation-State raises the question of compatibilty between the two, and if this is not possible the question becomes which is and/or will become the dominant power, the multinational corporation or the nation State ? Thus the fundamental dilemma of the modern State is how to retain national control over the effective implementation of domestic economic and political policies while keeping allowance for the openness of boundaries for multinational corporations to operate.

POWER STRUCTURE OF THE MNCs AND THE DEVELOPING ECONOMY

Concern over the management of the multinationals in the under-developed world is much greater problem than in the developed countries. The importance of foreign investment in the developing countries varies from country to country. In some countries it is relatively insignificant, whereas in others it plays a key role. Five countries alone—Brazil, Mexico, Venezuela,

Indonesia and Nigeria account for 36 per cent of all private foreign investment. Nine others—India, Malaysia, Argentina, Singapore, Peru, Hongkong, the Philippines, Trinidad and Tobago and Iran account for another 22 per cent.[7] Power of the MNCs grows out of their structural position within the relatively small and under-developed economies of many Southern States.[8] Because much of the GNP of under-developed States still comes from the agriculture and service sectors, MNCs contribute a relatively small part in total GNP. But foreign investment often accounts for important percentages of the total stock of local investment, local production and sales.[9] The net flow of foreign direct investment (FDI) in Brazil and Mexico have increased from 225 million and 196 million US dollars respectively in 1969 to 2223 million and 668 million US dollars respectively in 1979.[10]

More importantly, foreign investment dominates key industries in the developing countries. Historically firms from Northern hemisphere controlled the South's raw materials, the key to development. Multinationals, for example, controlled oil in the Middle East, copper in Chile and Zambia and bauxite in Jamaica and Guyana. Although less developed countries in some cases have increased control over these raw materials but still the Northern hemisphere firms retain control over a vast amount of Southern hemisphere primary products, and investment from the North has grown in this sector.

Second and most important recent area of control is manufacturing. After the second world war a desire of industrialisation by the developing countries have given more incentives to the MNCs. Foreign investment is growing more rapidly in manufacturing than the LDCs manufacturing sector as a whole—and thus dominating them. Foreign investment in the third world

---

7. United Nations, "Transnational Corporations in World Development : A Re-examination." New York, UNO, 1978, p. 254.
8. For a similar analysis of two countres, See Newfarmer, Richard S. and Mueller, Willard F., 'Multinational Corporations in Brazil and Mexico ; Structural Sources of Economic and Non-economic Power,' Report to the Sub-Committee on MNCs of the Committee on Foreign Relations, 94th Congress, 1st Session, Washington D.C. 1975.
9. See for example, Vernon, R., "Sovereignty at Bay" : The Multinational Spread of US Enterprises", Basic Books, New York, 1971, p. 22.
10. Mehdi, Salehizadeh, "Multinational Companies and Developing Countries : A New Relationship", Third World Quarterly, January 1983, Vol. 5, No. 1, p. 135.

tends to be found in the industries which are dominated by a small number of large firms. For example, US foreign investment is found in such highly concentrated industries as petroleum, copper, aluminium, chemicals, transportation, food products and machinery.[11] The large firms which dominate such industries have greater power to control supply and price than firms in more competitive industries. Thus the oligopolistic structure of the foreign investment means that significant economic power is concentrated in the hands of a few large firms.

These characteristics of the MNCs in the third world economies are :

(a) their important share of the overall economy ;

(b) their dominant position in key industries ; and

(c) the pre-dominance of oligopolistic firms ; mean that foreign firms are in a position to make decisions which have an important impact on the level and direction of development of the host economies. Furthermore, when local dominance by multinationals is combined with other characteristics of the MNCs, the stage is set for vast potential corporate power in the developing countries—economic as well as political. The integration of powerful local subsidiaries into huge international firms which are often world wide oligopolies and the centralisation of decision-making in the parent firms mean that many decisions crucial to the development of the less developed economies are not even made locally by the foreign firms but are made in the board rooms in New York or Tokyo.

The extent of corporate power can be understood by taking the examples of Brazil and Mexico as studied by Newfarmer and Mueller. The pattern of the foreign investment and its relationship to the economies of these two States reflect the constraints on decision-making characteristic of many less developed countries.

In Mexico, MNCs produced 23 per cent of total GDP in manufacturing ; 28 per cent of all Mexican sales (Newfarmer and

---

11. UNCTAD, 'Restrictive Business Practices, The Operation of Multinational Enterprises in Developing Countries, Their Role in Trade and Development', A study by Reymond Vernon, New York, UN, 1972, p. 3.

Mueller, 1975). In Brazil MNCs controlled 29 per cent of all assets in the manufacturing sector and produced 44 per cent of all local sales in the manufacturing industry.[12]

In both the countries control has been the greatest in the largest firms and certain key industries. In Mexico 50 per cent of three hundred largest industrial firms and 61 per cent of hundred largest firms were controlled. Foreign control is particularly predominant in the most technologically advanced and capital intensive industries in Mexico ; for example, in non-electrical machinery (95 per cent), transportation (79 per cent) and chemicals (68 per cent).[13] These industries are also the fastest growing and the most profitable.[14] Finally, foreign investment is found in concentrated industries. MNCs accounted for 71 per cent of all manufacturing sales in highly concentrated industries.[15]

The situation in Brazil is similar. 40 per cent of three hundred largest manufacturing firms and 59 per cent of top hundred manufacturing firms were foreign owned.[16] Foreign control is concentrated in the most advanced and most dynamic growth industries ; chemicals (69 per cent), transportation (84 per cent) and machinery (74 per cent).[17]

In both the countries they are integrated with international corporations. Local subsidiaries are owned directly by the parent, depend on the parent for finance and do most of their trading with the parent corporation.[18] The predominant position of foreign firms in these two countries means that decisions crucial for economic development are being made outside these countries and thus subjugating the entire government machinery and interfering with the priorities of economic development.

Another important problem has been the multinational's ability to intervene in the domestic political process of the host

---

12. UN, 'Transnational Corporations', p. 271 and UN Economic Commission for Latin America, Tendencias y Cambios en la inversion de las empresas internacionales en las paises en desarrollo y particularmente en America Latina, Santiago, Chile, UN 1978, pp. 70-71.
13. Newfarmer, Richard S. and Mueller, Willard F., 'Multinational Corporations in Brazil and Mexico', p. 54.
14. *Ibid.*, pp. 80-94.
15. *Ibid.*, p. 61.
16. *Ibid.*, p. 107.
17. *Ibid.*, p. 108.
18. *Ibid.*, pp. 73-80, 125-131.

State, to further corporate, as opposed to host government, interests. MNCs are potentially able to use their resources in both
legal and illegal political activities in host countries. Tactics such
as public relations activities, campaign contributions, bribery and
economic boycott are adopted by these corporations. In their
ability to intervene in domestic politics, the MNCs are, in one
sense, no different from national corporations ; the problem they
pose is not in the area of foreign investment but in their ability
as private corporations to influence the government. In fact, the
involvement of MNCs in local politics is a great challenge to
national sovereignty.

The MNCs are not only pursuing their economic objectives
but their political objectives also. The MNCs are not only violating the norms in the host countries but also violating the norms
set by the international agencies like the UNO. It has been
observed in many cases that the multinational corporations have
been used as a powerful instruments for furthering the foreign
policy by parent countries, especially in the case of US multinationals.

CLASHING WITH NATIONAL SOVEREIGNTY—SOME
CASES IN POINT

One of the significant directives by the UN and emphasised
frequently in current human relations is the principle of respect
for human rights and fundamental freedoms. The Charter of
Economic Rights and Duties of States called for respect for
human rights and fundamental freedom. The 31st General
Assembly adopted a number of resolutions linking the domination
of the politics of aparthied pursued by the government of South
Africa, to the activities of the MNCs. The Group of Eminent
Persons had themselves specifically recommended that both
the home and host countries should ensure through appropriate
action the MNCs did not violate sanctions imposed by the UNO
Security Council on countries suppressing human rights and
following racist policies.[19] It was, therefore, incumbent upon home
and host countries to see that UN resolutions, which imposed

19. The UN Document E/5500/Rev. 1 ; ST/ESA/6, "The Impact of MNCs
    on Development and International Relations", New York, 1974, p. 50.

sanctions against South Africa and Southern Rhodesia and called upon all the members of the UN to apply economic sanctions, were duly observed. The Bingham Inquiry Report revealed, while the British Government spent millions of pound sterling blockading the Port of Beira to prevent oil reaching Rhodesia, a number of international oil companies including the British Petroleum in which government itself had a majority share, were supplying oil to the illegal regime of Rhodesia by land. The irony of it was that Shell, which produced a Code of Ethics for the MNCs, was itself involved in this violation. Its subsidiary, the Shell Mojambique, jointly owned by British Petroleum, either directly or through swap arrangement, with the French Group, supplied oil overland to Rhodesia for a decade after 1966. What was surprising in this case was that there were two government directors on the board of the British Petroleum.

Political intervention exercised by the MNCs may be direct or indirect. It may be direct as happened in Chile, where Allende was overthrown by the International Telegraph and Telephones Corporation (a US multinational) or political involvement by the United Fruits (again a US multinational) in Guatemala in the 1950s or Union Mineir in Katanga in 1960s. Bedak revolt of Sumatra in Indonesia was also linked with nationalisation of Royal Dutch Shell's holdings.[20]

Indirect political interventions are more subtle and create at times, very peculiar situations. For developed countries the MNCs are powerful instrument of their foreign policy. For example, the Hickenlooper Amendment to the US Foreign Assistance Act, requiring the President of the United States to stop aid to countries expropriating US property without prompt and effective compensation was introduced in the US Senate on the initiative of Harold Geneen, the then president of the ITT whose utilities subsidiaries were being threatened in Brazil and Argentina. After the amendment was passed in 1962, Nicaragua was told that the amendment would be applied against it if the land reforms legislation, that would have affected the US fruit plantation, were proceeded with. In 1963, Senator Hickenlooper re-wrote the amendment so that it could be directed specifically against

---

20. See Economic Times, Bombay, January 3, 1976.

Argentina's decision to change the contracts of US oil companies. US oil was also cut off in 1963, for three years to peru, without even formally invoking the amendment, to force Fernando Belaunde Terry to settle with the International Petroleum Corporation, an affiliate of Exxon. In 1963 in Sri Lanka, when the Bandarnayake's government proceeded to take over the operation of Caltex and Stamac and the compensation was found inadequate, the Hickenlooper amendment was invoked to cut off aid to Sri Lanka. The aid was resumed only after the Bandarnayake's government was defeated and Dudley Senanayake took over in 1965.[21]

In 1972, US Ambassador to Jamaica, Vincent De Roulet, threatened financial reprisal if nationalisation in the bauxite industry was put up as an issue in the Jamaican Presidential campaign. In this, he was aided by Gonzalez amendment to Foreign Assistance Act which, *inter alia*, stipulated the nomination of an American representative in the Inter American Development Bank to vote against loans to countries that expropriated American property.[22]

The role played by the ITT has been brilliantly brought out by Anthony Sampson in his book 'The Sovereign State : The Secret History of ITT' (London, 1974) which details the activities of the ITT not only in Chile, but in other countries of Latin America as well. In December 1972, when Allende came to address UN General Assembly in New York he stated that "the ITT had driven its tentacles deep into my country and proposed to manage our political life. I accuse the ITT of attempts to bring about civil war." He also attached other big corporations which, he said, "had been cunningly and terrifyingly effective in preventing us from exercising our rights as sovereign State."[23]

The ITT is not a solitary example. Political interference of the MNCs in the internal affairs of the host countries could be traced to the United Fruits Co. in Latin America, direct political

---

21. The Economic Times, January 3, 1976.
22. See Rubin, Seymor J., "The Multinational Enterprises and the Home State" in 'Global Companies' (ed.) by George Ball, Prentice Hall, New Jersey, Englewood, 1975.
23. Sampson, Anthony, p. 235.

interference of Firestone since 1926 in Liberia, the detailed involvement of Belgian Union Mineire in Congolese politics, Shell's participation in the operations of Nigerian government during closing stages of civil war with Baifra and others.[24]

The Fortune of August 1975, gives many instances where MNCs bribed their way into political favours of their host countries. For instance, Exxon contributed $ 27 million for Italian election fund and allowed the Italian subsidiaries to give away $ 19 million more in dubious ways and condoned falsification of its record. The United Brand bribed a Honduras's Cabinet Minister to cut a crushing banana tax to half. Gulf made a pay off of $ 3,50,000 in Bohemia and also gave a helicopter worth of $ 1.10 lakhs to the President of Bohemia who was ironically killed when the helicopter crashed. The Gulf which was the biggest investor in South Korea having put in $ 360 million into fertiliser and petro-chemical partnership with the South Korean Government contributed $ 1 million to the President P. Cheng Hee's political party. In 1970, the party's fund raiser, Kim, demanded $ 10 million more. Bob R. Dorsey, the chief executive of the Gulf haggled him down to $ 3 million which according to Dorsey's calculation was adequate to run the 1971 election in that small country.

SOME INDIAN CASES IN POINT

As suggested earlier the main concern of the study is to highlight mainly the Indian experiences with the working of the MNCs, of course, with international substantiation.

There have been many allegations made inside and outside the Parliament about the functioning of the MNCs in India. The statement of Mr. Vidya Prakash Dutt, Member Parliament, was important in the Rajya Sabha on May 14, 1975 giving the details about the *modus operandi* of these MNCs quoting extensively from the New York Times of 11th May 1975. The truth of the allegation is borne out by the Report of the Parliamentary Joint Committee on the Foreign Contribution (Regulations) Bill, 1973. The Committee specifically brought in the MNCs in the bill whose activities in the political arena were examined in greater detail

---

24. Stephenson, Hugh, "The Coming Clash", p. 54.

at the time the evidence were taken by the Committee. Kalyan Rai Chandrappan and J. Rai, members of the Committee observed in this connection.

"The closest ally of the CIA is MNCs which use various means to corrupt and subvert the independence and territorial integrity and economy of the countries where they operate. With tremendous financial powers at their command and their firm grip over raw materials and minerals and other resources of the third world countries, they are continuously trying to maintain their hold through massive financial support to anti-democratic elements and have become States within State. Under cover of trade and business, they attempt to infiltrate into every layer of society and resort to every possible means including financial assistance to influence the politics of the countries where they operate. They are highest single menace to independence and democratic forms of government which are trying hard to delink themselves from the stranglehold of colonial economy."[25]

A General fear is that the CIA agents are operating through the MNCs covertly under the commercial cover agreements.[26] Two important cases are worth noting here to show how the MNCs are trying to influence the government policies and implementation of such policies by officials by indulging in corrupt practices. It came to be known that M/s Phillips Petroleum Co. of the USA and Good year (India) Ltd. were making illegal payments and political contributions.

Case of Goodyear Tyre (India) Ltd.

In case of the Goodyear Tyre (India) Ltd., the Securities and Exchange Commission of the USA filed before the District Court in Columbia a case against the company for such offence.[27] The statement filed by the Goodyear Tyre (India) Ltd. has confessed that—

---

25. Joint Committee, Rajya Sabha (1-15), The Foreign Contribution (Regulation) Bill, p. 17.

26. Times of India, New Delhi, May 15, 1975.

27. Securities and Exchange Commission *Vs.* The Good year Tyre and Rubber Company, District Court of Columbia (Case 77-2167 dated 21st December, 1977) also Goodyear (India) Ltd., Annual Report 1977, para 13 .

"(a) the Indian subsidiary of the company had been maintaining funds which had not been recorded in the books of the company ;

(b) these funds were derived largely from rebates from suppliers of raw materials reflecting the difference between the minimum price fixed by the government and the market price ;

(c) estimates of the total amount in the fund during its existence over a period of five years from 1971-75 varied from $ 5 lakhs to $ 8 lakhs. The precise amount at any particular point of time was not ascertainable ;

(d) the fund was utilised for a variety of purposes including payment of minor foreign government officials to assure an adequate supply of raw materials, police protection and to secure government business...payment to labour officials to settle problems, for political contributions and for the financing of employees' travels, school and moving expenses."

Case of Phillips Petroleum

As regards Phillips Petroleum[28] revelations before a grand jury in the United States in September 1976 and earlier disclosures pressed for by the US Securities Exchange commission brought to light the possibility of one million dollar pay off to Indian nationals in connection with the negotiation and construction of the Cochin Refinery in the sixties. Giving details of the judgment of the grand jury at Tulsa, Oklahoma State, relating to tax evasion by the Phillips Petroleum 'Co. the report said that $ 4.4 lakhs were paid by Cochin Refinery Ltd. each year for three years, 1969-71 and Phillips Petroleum put this money in numbered Swiss accounts. This money, the Tulsa grand jury said, was then transmitted to a Panama subsidiary of Phillips Petroleum for disbursement to certain foreign associates of the company and not properly recorded on the company's books of financial accounts.

---

28. USA *Vs.* Phillips Petroleum Co. (CR No. 76—CR—117 dated 5th July 1977), District Court for Northern District of Oklahoma.

Other Cases

These are again not the solitary examples. ICI, a dominating chemical firm, in a statement filed before the Securities and Exchange Commission admitted having made "some payments directly or indirectly to government officials in other areas of the world (other than UK, Europe, North America, Australia and Japan)."[29] This averaged $ 3 lakhs a year. Alkali and Chemical Corporation of India, a subsidiary of ICI, was a recipient of duty concession of Rs. 240 crores on its import of Ethyl Alcohol and its case for duty concession was stated to have been sponsored by the West Bengal Government and by the then Minister of Petroleum and Chemicals in the Government of India.[30]

The Group of Eminent Persons in their report unequivocally condemned the "subversive political interventions on the part of the multinationals directed towards the overthrow and substitution of the host country governments or fostering an internal or international situation that stimulates the conditions for such action." But the political intervention of MNCs does not differ from that of large national firms. The only question is that the sovereignty of the host countries is at stake. This problem is probably due to the ill-defined or undefined 'permissible public activities' of the multinational corporations.

The operations of the MNCs have, no doubt, generated misunderstanding and tensions with the governments and people of host countries. As corporate citizens of many nations engaged in transnational business, they confront conflicts between national policies and divergent economic and social systems and values. As agents of technological and cultural change they naturally provide critical reactions from businessmen and governments.

The MNCs are international manifestation of economic imperialism. US multinationals are subject to more criticism because they constitute the biggest part of all the international firms taken together, and therefore, supposed to be the best propagandists for a certain conception of the 'New World Order' demanded by the US imperialists. Japanese and European com-

---

29. The Statesman, New Delhi, September 22, 1976.
30. 5th Lok Sabha, PAC 172 Report, pp. 14-15

panies whose interest would be served by a world without trade barriers, prove themselves faithful allies of the US firms and the American government. They are all participants in a capitalist system which must be international if it is to flourish. The time has come for finding the answers of highly legitimate questions about the MNCs.

Why do they grow faster than other companies ?

At whose expenses ?

What world are they shaping for us ?

Are they politically neutral ?

Is their growth compatible with the national interest ?

Who has ultimate control over the actions of their subsidiaries ?

If national independence still possible ?

Looking to all these mind boggling situations and the questions posed by the operation of the MNCs one is inclined to make certain suggestions though of limited scope. It has been an established fact that the multinational corporations are directly or indirectly, overtly or covertly, clashing with the national sovereignty. These are taking advantage of the developing countries of their being soft States. Looking to the ramifications and magnitude of their political overtones it has become not only an economic but a political necessity to curb their activities. Now there is high time to think about the choice between the sovereignty and multinationals. The age of political expediency of allowing the multinationals in the developing countries is now gone. Political dominance of foreign rule is over only conceptually but in practice the economic dominance by foreign multinationals has proved to be the political lever which is still dominating the less developed countries invisibly. These subtilities are at times beyond the understanding of human capacity but at the same time it is the landmark of the human ingenuity to subjugate the nations with more dexterity through the instrumentality of the multinationals.

SUGGESTIONS

Political aspects of the MNCs are not easy to solve nor they are likely to be solved immediately because this problem is not only political in the strict sense of the term but more of a mental, a problem of deep rooted prejudice, predilection and perception. Whatever we have inherited was accepted like destiny and the hangover still continues. Most of the foreign brands, though not all, still command an eughoria even in the best of minds. We never couraged to have a fundamental departure from the beaten track, nor we showed any tendency to do it. Thus the problem has gone deeper. Moreover, the political will is scarcely evident, if not totally absent, to solve the menace. Some suggestions may be advanced here to break the ice.

1. There should be a complete restriction on the entrance of multinational corporations. Hundred per cent indigenous firms and technology should be preferred. Though this may give an extremistic feeling but the countries will have to do it as China did in its early stages of development. Multinational Corporations should be allowed only when a country's economic is in a self sustaining stage of growth. The fact is that even the developed countries of today restricted such foreign investments in their countries to protect their economies. For example, the Australian government's Committee of Economic Enquiry recommended to the Parliament in September 1965 to limit the 'new overseas investment' to an annual level of $ 336 million. The French government's policy of curtailing new foreign affiliates in 1963 was directed largely against the potential dominance of particular industry sectors, Japan not only restricted the aggregate inflow of foreign equity but also effectively kept foreign investors out of 'strategic' and 'key industries such as electricals, chemicals and automobiles.[31] Such restrictions would be effective reducing tensions arising from the spread of multinational enterprises.[32]

2. If the foreign collaboration is at all necessary the firms from and to the developing countries should be encouraged. Because most of the developing countries have nearly identical economic problems or developmental priorities. This will not only

---

31. Behrman, Jack N., 'National Interests and the Multinational Enterprises—Tensions among the North Atlantic Countries', Prentice Hall Inc., Englewood Cliffs, New Jersey, 1970, p. 134.
32. Leo Model has proposed that the enterprises restrain themselves in their overseas expansion to relieve the tension. "The Politics of Private Foreign Investment." Foreign Affairs, July 1967, pp. 639-51. But no company can afford to limit its expansion while others do not do so. Such actions would require concerted agreement and governmental sanction.

boost the developmental potentials of the less developed countries but also expand and develop the markets and additional
generation of wealth and income will help these countries instead
of concentrating in the hands of few capitalist countries of the
world. The developing countries produce most of the world's raw
material and primary goods and this is again a favourable aspect
of forming the MNCs from developing countries. It should be very
well understood that the interest of developed nations and developing nations are bound to clash and so with the multinationals.

3. There should be a legislation for preventing the multinational from taking part in any type of political activity directly
or indirectly. If some multinational firm is found to have involved
in such activities it must be declared as *persona non grata* and
even its business activities must be declared illegal unequivocally.
There should be an independent body, with assertive rights, to
keep constant watch on the foreign firms' activities related to its
business or otherwise.

4. The governments of the less developed countries could use
one important bargaining advantage they possess—control over
access to their territory.[33] But the less developed countries being
the soft state this seems to be very difficult. One of the major
problems is that MNCs too have control over certain resources
required for the development of these countries. The less developed countries' desire for pseudo benefit of foreign direct investment posed an important dilemma for the policy makers. On the
one hand officials want to regulate the MNCs to maximise the
national benefits and to minimise the national costs. On the other
hand they do not want to make regulations so restrictive that it
will deter potential investor. Another factor weakening the
bargaining power of LDCs is the absence of competition for investment opportunities. Furthermore, it is said and felt by the
interested groups, that even if a country resolves the dilemma in
favour of regulation, their remain important constraints on the
ability of the country to carry out regulatory policies. But this
is the time when the economic administrators will have to choose
between the two. There should not be any compromising via-media
for such an enormous problem threatening the very sovereignty
of the nations.

---

33. Samuel, Huntington, "Transnational Corporations in the World Politics,'
    World Politics, April 25, 1973, pp. 333-368.

TRANSFER OF TECHNOLOGY AND MULTINATIONAL CORPORATIONS

Introduction

Structure of Technology in Developing Countries

Basic Characteristics of Transfer of Technology

The Form of Transfer of Technology

Restrictive Practices

Various Issues related to Transfer of Technology

    (a) Licence and Patents

    (b) R&D Activities in the Developing Countries

    (c) Adaptability of Products and Processes to Local Conditions

    (d) Linkage to the Host Country's Domestic Economy

Indian Engineering Industry—A Case Study

Case of Gabriel (India) Limited

Recent Cases of Transfer of Technology

Impact on Employment and Human Resource Development

Conclusions

Suggestions

3

Transfer of Technology and Multinational Corporations

INTRODUCTION

During various development decades the technology has been and is being considered as the most important factor for development. The less developed countries have been depending on the technology supplied by the developed countries and the former have been in continuous trap of the technological lure shown by the latter. Global Corporations (or Multinational Corportions) are the most powerful instrument of technology transfer to these countries by means of various package deals or otherwise. The central strategy of the global corporations is, irrespective of the country where technology is being transferred or so to say being dumped, that it will ensure stability, expansion and high profits for the planetary enterprises. The implementation of that strategy depends upon the control of three basic components of corporate power : finance capital, technology and market place ideology. The record of the past dozen years suggests clearly that the multinational corporation has used these components of power, as one might expect, to promote its growth and profitability. But it is these very strategies which have had an adverse effect on distribution of income and on employment levels in underdeveloped countries around the world.

The argument of development potentials in favour of Multinational Corporations regarding the transfer of technology has got to be judged while anwering the following questions.[1]

---

1. Prakash, Om, 'Economic Sins of the Nations,' Progressive Publishers, College Street, Calcutta, 1978, p. 246.

(a) How keen the MNCs are to share their know-how with the nationals of host countries ?

(b) How appropriate is the technology, that is sought to be shared, for the needs of the host economies ?

(c) How effective is the absorptive capacity of the techno-logy-importing country ?

(d) How satisfactory can be the arrangements and the terms for the transferance of technology ?

(e) Whether it is possible to develop comparable 'cross flows' of technology between the home and host economies on a 'near equality' basis ?

It this chapter only technology part of the total strategy and impact thereof is considered. It is seen that most of the technology supplied by the multinational corporations to the developing countries is to serve their own business or political interests instead of serving the cause of being the 'engines of development.' Rather the technology has become a source of economic exploitation in the developing countries on the one hand and these countries have become the junkyard for the obsolete technology of developed nations on the other. A form of technology transfer that has recently developed is transferred by licensing of patents and processes on a royalty basis. But the matter does not end here. Use of technology and information thereof is subject to so many strings on the part of developing countries, commonly known as 'restrictive business practices.' All the more the phrase 'sophisticated technology' has become a selling slogan by which the 'soft' developing world is easily attracted.

STRUCTURE OF TECHNOLOGY IN DEVELOPING COUNTRIES

Most of the underdeveloped countries in Latin America, Asia and Africa have already set in motion a process of growth along the classical path of capitalist development. Their growth exercise is very much similar to the process of industrialisation in the West particulary in terms of output and mechanical technology and human skills used. This pattern of industrialisation and also the use of highly capital intensive technology, though not demanded by the national circumstances, has been probably dictated by the institutionalisation of Western consumption values in elite groups.

Let us now examine the source of this technology. Data available are, however, inadequate and fragmentary for firm conclusions. It is nevertheless, not too difficult to judge on the basis of information provided by the United Nations[2] that the developing countries are virtually dependent upon the multinational corporations of the advanced countries of North America, Western Europe and Japan for their technology. An important study based on the survey of technology transfer contracts made by the multinational corporations with the national firms of five Andean Pact countries indicate that the absolute dependence is much more than is reflected in figures. Weighing the number of patents by their economic and technological worth (*i.e.*, volume of sales, or value added), Vaitsos in this study argues that most developing countries are likely to find that the (so) weighted patents belonging to their own nationals amount to only a fraction of one per cent of the total patents granted by such countries.[3] In addition to this, Vaitsos has observed a big concentration of control of technology. His study of Columbia has revealed that in chemicals, synthetic fibre and pharmaceutical industries ten per cent of all patent holders, all foreign multinational corporations, control 60 per cent of all patents.[4] This concentrated control of technology is probably the most effective weapon in the armoury of the multinational corporations to ensure oligopolistic conditions in the markets of under-developed countries to appropriate huge surplus which over a period may be repatriated to the parent developed countries.

Apart from the problem of concentrated control of technology, another basic issue that has to be settled is whether the

2. United Nations, 'The Role of Patents in Transfer of Technology to Developing Countries,' New York, 1964.
3. Vaitsos, Constantine, V., 'Patents Revisited : Their Functions in the Developing Countries, Journal of Development Studies, October 1972,
4. *Ibid.*

real need of labour surplus developing countries is to transfer advanced technologies from developed countries or to create
new intermediate technologies adapted to their specific conditions.
To us, there is a strong case for developing labour intensive technologies in all labour surplus backward economies particularly
looking to the almost negligible social opportunity cost of labour.
But the behaviour of American multinationals has been contrary
to this need of developing countries. Wickham Skinner's study[5]
of the technological strategy of the American multinationals has indicated that in practice the choice of techniques is seldom influenced
by the social welfare considerations of the host countries. Process
and equipments are rarely developed for the specific environment
in these economies and most of the companies without making a
careful analysis and study in their choice of technology have very
often exported them unchanged from domestic operations. It is
frequently argued that this singular rigidity on the part of multinationals in the use of technology is to a great extent due to the
conviction of their management that the familiar mechanised
techniques are superior to labour intensive ones. Facts, however,
do not support this contention. To us, it seems that the more
important reason for this lack of flexibility in the attitude of
multinationals is their desire to ensure oligopolistic power in
markets of the developing countries. Secondary reason is also
there. MNCs dislike dealing with large number of workers and
their housing, welfare and social security needs. Jan Tinbergen
ascribes this preference of multinational corporations for highly
capital intensive techniques to their lack of awareness with
regard to various technological alternatives which exist in planning for industrial activities in the developing countries.[6]

BASIC CHARACTERISTICS OF TRANSFER OF TECHNOLOGY

It has already been noted that the total influx of technology
in the developing countries is from the advanced countries. To be
able to understand its implications, we have to take note of the
two basic characteristics of technology transfer. First, the prin-

---

5. Skinner, Wickham, 'American Industry in the Developing Economies,'
   1968, pp. 140-141.
6. Tinbergen, Jan, 'Choice of Technology and Industrial Planning,' Industrialisation and Productivity Bulletin, No. 1, April 1958.

cipal instrument of technology transfer are multinational corporations which either through their subsidiaries or through the contractual transactions made with the developing countries bring mechanised processes and equipments not locally available. Very often the terms and conditions of technology transfer are arbitrarily settled under highly imperfect market conditions by the technology supplying MNCs. The monopolistic strength of the technology suppliers emanates from the patents protection for differentiated products and processes, the integration of market for technology with the monopolistic market for technology embodying inputs and the weak bargaining power of buyers who have neither access to information about alternative technologies and their sources nor the necessary infra-structure to evaluate the appropriateness of equipments, intermediates and processes.[7]

Second, the large part of the influx of technology in the developing countries is in response to the policy of industrialisation through import substitution. In developing countries, due to structural factors and their consequential effects on terms of trade[8] much reliance cannot be placed on exports to transfer savings into current investment goods.[9] Naturally, a deliberate strategy of creating a tariff wall to overcome the foreign exchange difficulties has to be followed, and this provides an incentive to the multinationals to move to developing countries with their unaltered plants and technical know-how to manufacture import restricted goods for sale in local elite markets. Whatever may be the advantages of this transfer to the multinationals, its disadvantages to the host countries are quite obvious. Furthermore, it is a gross or crude fitting of technology to circumstances, and the fit may be random.

THE FORM OF TRANSFER OF TECHNOLOGY

Transfer of technology from the developed countries to developing ones is made in number of ways. But for convenience sake

---

7. Subramaniam, K.K., 'Problems of Technology Transfer from Advanced to Developing Countries', Paper presented at the International Seminar on Technology Transfer held on 11-13 December, 1972, organised by the Council of Scientific and Industrial Research, New Delhi.
8. Emmanuel, Asghiri, 'Unequal Exchange', Monthly Review Press, New York, 1972.
9. Patel, S. J., 'Depressed Exports : The Hard Core of Development Problems', Economic Internationale, Agosto-November, 1971.

they are broadly classified into two categories, *viz.*, direct mechanism and indirect mechanism.[10] The direct mechanism includes the transfer of technology through banks, journals, industrial fairs, technical co-operation, movement of skilled people, etc. This necessarily demands initiative on the part of indigenous enterprises in making the selection of appropriate technologies. This, however, is not the principal form of import of technology in the developing countries. The indirect mechanism implies technology transfer in a 'package' or a 'bundle' containing technology embodying equipments, industrial properties like patents and trade marks, skill, equity capital, etc. In this system a local enterprise negotiates with some multinational for import of various elements of technology in a 'package' and the terms and conditions are settled through the process of commercial transaction. Since the trading partners in this case are unequal, the terms and conditions are invariably restrictive and the price extracted for the technology unreasonably high. However, the position may be different if the government of the technology buying country intervenes effectively. In any case, the mechanism makes the local enterprise completely dependent on the multinationals for the supply of technology in future. MNC, the principal supplier of technology in the package form, has an obvious preference for indirect mechanism, because it provides scope for monopolistic practices and also for controlling the industrial structure of the host countries. The buyers of technology accept this mechanism for their own reasons. A probable reason one can think of is the lack of adequate R & D infra-structure in the country concerned to provide a continuous flow of technology. But to use non-technological factors like, expectations of high profits from foreign patents, brand names, trade marks, etc., and availability of tied foreign credit appears to be rather more important reason for importing technology in package form.

RESTRICTIVE PRACTICES

Apart from the fact that most of the technology transferred to the developing countries by the MNCs has been crudely

---

10. UNCTAD. 'The Channels of Mechanisms of the Transfer of Technology from Developed to Developing Countries', TD/B/AC. II. 5.

fitted to the economic environment there, the actual gain to the recipients of technology is much less than its potential face value due to various restrictive conditions invariably imposed on them by the suppliers. But this hardly influences the decisions of the entrepreneurs belonging to the developing countries who are always too eager to collaborate with multinationals with the objective of maximising their private benefit even if it conflicts with the larger interest of the country. The restrictive clauses which appear in contracts of technology transfer nonetheless, raise important issues about the way multinationals curtail the sovereignity of consumers and thereby undermine the economic and social interests of the host countries.

Let us now examine the nature of restrictions. One of the most common restrictive clauses in contracts of technology transfers is that of export prohibition. In other words, foreign technology using national firms and subsidiaries of the multinational obtain equipments and technical know-how on the specific condition that the production will be done only for domestic market. In rare cases multinationals grant freedom to technology consumers in respect of exports. An UNCTAD study in 1969 had revealed that restrictive practices had been observed in the Latin American, Asian and African countries without exception in the process of purchase of foreign technology.[11] In India where some awareness of the various issues involved in technology transfer and their implications exist, the government intervention has resulted in reducing the burden of restrictive clauses. The RBI survey of 1969 and 1974 found that in spite of regulation of technical collaborations, a large number of restrictionist clauses did get through in almost half of technology transfer contracts. To be specific, of these 52 per cent related to demarcation of the countries to which exports were permitted and about 33 per cent to stipulations regarding 'permission of collaborators for exports'. Clauses enforcing a total ban on exports figured only in 8 per cent of agreements with export restrictions."[12] In Latin American Andean Pact countries, where MNCs are well entrenched practices are widespread. A study covering Bolivia, Columbia, Ecuador, Peru and Chile has analysed 451 contracts of which 409 contained

11. UNCTAD, 'Restrictive Business Practices' TD/B/C2/93 1969, pp. 4-6.
12. RBI, 'Foreign Collaboration in Indian Industry', RBI Bulletin, January 1969, p. 22.

information on export restrictive practices. After a careful examination of the various terms and conditions laid down in these contracts, it was concluded that whereas in Chile 72 per cent of the contracts prohibited exports totally, the position in Bolivia, Columbia, Ecuador and Peru was much worse. In these four countries taken together about 81 per cent of the contracts restricted exports totally and another 5 per cent partially.[13] The implications of these restrictive clauses in backward economies are serious. First, by virtue of these restrictive provisions technology supplier multinationals exercise control over the business decisions of the technology buyers in respect of output, market prices, and often this results in creation of excess capacity. Secondly, restrictions forbidding sales in third markets inhibit host country's export promotion drive and thereby prove to be a serious obstacle to development.

A large number of technology transfer contracts include obligatory conditions with regard to purchase of equipment and intermediate goods from the same source as that of technical know-how.[14] For technology supplying MNCs such tie-in arrangements serve an important purpose. They ensure a secure market for their equipments and intermediates and facilitate the earning of monopoly profits. Tie-in restrictive arrangements in technology transfer contracts take several forms. The most common form is to explicitly forbid the purchase of capital goods and intermediate inputs from other sources. Sometimes, in addition to this, use of local materials is either limited or even completely prohibited. Wherever these explicit restrictive practices are being resented by the Governments of technology buying countries, the MNCs achieve similar results in the purchase of intermediate goods through clauses on quality control. It is, however, notable that one does not encounter any tie-in arrangement between foreign companies and their parents in advanced countries.

---

13. Vaitsos, C.V., 'Inter-country Income Distribution and Transnational Enterprises', Oxford, 1974.
14. Gruber, W., Mehta, F. and Vernon, R., 'The R&D Factor in International Investment of United States Industry', Journal of Political Economy, Autumn, 1966.

VARIOUS ISSUES RELATED TO THE TRANSFER OF TECHNOLOGY

Many facets could be considered for discussing the phenomena of technology transfer from multinational corporations to the developing countries. The issues relevant to our analysis and touched upon here are as under :

(a) License and Patents

(b) Research and Development activities in developing countries

(c) Adaptability of products and processes to the local conditions

(d) Linkage to the host country's domestic economy.

(a) License and Patents

Many developing countries regard the purchase of technology through licensing arrangements without equity participation by the foreign owner of the technology, as a highly desirably way of bringing about a transfer of technology while minimising loss of control of economic activity. In India the system of acquiring foreign technology on the basis of license and patents is a recent trend for the direct equity participation has not been so welcome in recent years, particularly after midseventies. At the other end of the spectrum, wholly owned subsidiaries may not pay separately for technology through royalties and technical fees because the benefits of technology accrue to the parent firm in the form of the subsidiaries' earnings and the dividends paid to the parent. In the case of partial equity ownership by the transnationals the separate payment for royalties and fees for parent company technology is quite common.

The host countries' principal concerns with respect to the purchase of technology, whether patented or unpatented, are the price charged and the restrictive conditions attached to the licensing agreements. There is a tendency to regard technology as being sold under monopolistic or oligopolistic conditions and hence as being overpriced (the problem of overpricing is being discussed in a separate chapter). Moreover, the royalties paid for technology are seen as excessive in relation to the transfer costs because the expenses incurred by the transnational corporations in designing or developing it have already been sunk. Perhaps the most serious concern, however, relates to the restrictive clauses commonly included in licensing agreements. Among these deemed most objectionable are the clauses obliging the licensee to purchase materials or equipments from the licensor (often at exorbitant prices), limitations of sales to the domestic market or to designated foreign markets and grant-back provisions (*i.e.*, provisions that give the licensor all rights to improvements).

(b) Research and Development Activities in the Developing Countries

The foreign technology is regarded in developing countries as inappropriate, high priced and subject to restrictive conditions, many developing countries have sought to reduce their dependence on imports of technology by encouraging the development of an indigenous R & D capacities. However, if there is no existing domestic core of R and D facilities, the effort can be frustrating. Apart from the high costs, there is brain drain, that is, the tendency of the scientists and engineers to migrate from poor to rich countries not only because of higher salaries but also because of wider contracts, more ample infra-structure of equipments and publication facilities and more advantages.

The multinationals have shown little interest in countering these tendencies by establishing superficial R and D facilities in the developing countries where they operate. But generally they have shown a strong preference for locating such facilities at home or in other developed countries and for concentrating on the kinds of products and processes appropriate to their own needs rather than to the developing countries.

(c) Adaptability of Products and Processes to Local Conditions

In developing countries due to such technology transfer the goods produced and the processes adopted in producing thereof is inappropriate. Too sophisticated, too highly designed and too elaborately packaged to meet the needs of the poor masses, such products cater largely to the needs of the consumption demand of the elite. It is sometimes observed, however, that undesirable consumption pattern may in a fundamental sense be more a reflection of an existing uneven distribution of wealth, income and privilege in developing countries than of the effects of the activities of foreign firms. But the facts have proved contrary to this.

A related and perhaps more important issue is the appropriateness of the production processes used by the foreign firms. In particular, they are excessively capital intensive in relation to the abundance of cheap labour in developing countries. In such situation this intensifies the employment problem, aggravate inequalities of income, worsen the balance of payment by excessive importation of capital equipments and even bias the output towards excessively sophisticated products. Transplantation of western technologies have proved disastrous by disturbing the whole production structure of the developing economy. Non-adaptability of such technologies and their products have proved socially and economically costly.

(d) Linkage to the Host Country's Domestic Economy

Developing countries have been asserting that certain foreign operations have an enclave character, that is, they have few backward or forward linkages to the domestic economy. Backward linkages are the purchase of local inputs ; forward linkages are the domestic use of the firm's output in further productive operations. The multinational corporations are working both sides and accruing the economies of scale of a high standard. This sort of working of these multinational corporations are possible only because of their oligopolistic nature and the resources at their command—both economic and political. Thus the linkage go in favour of these multinational firms to the detriment of the ultimate concern of the third world.

CASE STUDY OF THE INDIAN ENGINEERING GOODS INDUSTRY

This is a sector where foreign ownership and control have accompanied the transfer of technology in a substantial way.[15]

---

15. See RBI Surveys on Foreign Collaborations.

Whichever measure one may use, it is evident that the Indian engineering industry is very much dependent on the technology from developed countries. For the purpose of analysis 60 units were studied and divided in four different clusters (for clusters see Appendix II)—Cluster I—of high foreign association having majority foreign holding ; Cluster II—of medium foreign association having joint venture with foreign minority ownership control ; Cluster III—low foreign association having Indian majority or full ownership with formal technical collaboration agreements with foreign firms ; and Cluster IV—no foreign association having Indian firms with no foreign capital and technology import.[16]

The export performance of the engineering industry was assessed on the basis of the composite index combining the following two indicators :—

1. proportion of output that is exported.

2. rate of growth of the share of export in the total contribution.

Formula used for the purpose is :

$$EP = \sqrt[n-1]{\frac{Et}{El}} \quad \frac{\sum\limits_{t=1}^{n} tPt}{\sum\limits_{t=1}^{n}}$$

Where, Et = export in year 1, 2, 3, 4
El = export in 1970-71
Pt = share in the production exported in year t, Pt is weighted, (the weights varying from 1 to 4).

It is seen that the domestic firms with relatively low degree of foreign association have performed comparatively better in export performance than the firms with high degree of foreign association. The export performance index (or the export co-efficient) of foreign subsidiaries was found to be the lowest (0.0348) whereas that of Indian firms with little foreign association was found to be the highest (0.1017). In such a situation it seems

---

16. For detail study see Subrahmanian, K.K. and Pillai, P. Mohan, 'Multi-nationals and Indian Exports', Allied Publishers, New Delhi, 1979.

true that multinational corporations supplying technology are less interested in export market and more with the orientation of domestic market (the host country market).

At the same time the import intensity of these Clusters are also calculated again by a pioneering study of Subrahmanian and Pillai. Import intensity is measured in terms of the import share in a rupee of raw materials consumption of manufacturing firms in the different clusters, of foreign association. It is calculated that foreign subsidiaries are characterised by high import intensity (or import coefficient) and low export coefficient. The import coefficient of foreign subsidiaries was the highest (0.2061) while for the Indian firms was the lowest (0.1128). This high import coefficient has been contributed by the capital intensive technology adopted by the multinational corporations. At the same time a good cost is paid by the host countries for this foreign technology (apart from its obsolescence) is in terms of 'adaptation pinpricks'.

The overall trade impact has also been dismal. For both the Clusters I and II the net foreign exchange earnings was stated to be negative.

THE CASE OF GABRIEL (INDIA) LIMITED[17]

The Company was promoted in 1961 by the Gabriel Company, USA and Anands with 50 : 50 share holding, to manufacture and distribute shock absorbers in India. The Company has a spectacular record of growth. From 1961 to 1977 its sales have increased by more than 15 times, networth has also multiplied by fifteen times, one equity share of Rs. 100 has grown to Rs. 1,200 and an average divided of 21 per cent has been paid. The foreign share holders have shared half of the prosperity. It has recently diluted its foreign ownership from 48.9 per cent to 39.1 per cent under the FERA. The Gabriel Co. Cleveland, Ohio, USA the foreign shareholder of Gabriel India Ltd., is a multinational company which was acquired by the Maremont Corporation, USA in 1963. Maremont manufactures and distributes ordnance material, machined parts and electrical parts and provides marketing

---

17. Swami, Dalip S., 'Multinational Corporations and the World Economy,' Alps (International) Publishers, 1980, New Delhi.

channel to extensive lines of foreign car parts purchased from foreign manufacturers. It has major manufacturing operations in Canada, Italy, Venezuela, Argentina, Mexico and South Africa.

The company has entered into financial and technical collaboration with Federal Mogul (FM) Corporation, Southfield, Michigan, USA. The terms and conditions of the financial and technical collaboration with FM will show how the host countries are paying for the transfer of technology. The Collaboration Agreement provides that the Gabriel India Ltd. will sell in cash its equity shares worth of Rs. 36.96 lakhs to FM, which will amount to 14 per cent of the company's paid up capital as increased in 1978. In exchange of this 14 per cent ownership of the Company FM has entered into a License Agreement[18] which provides for :

(*a*) the grant by FM to the Company of a License to manufacture, process, assemble, use and sell the licensed products in India under Federal Mogul's Current Patents and export the same throughout the world, except USA, France, Italy, Spain, Argentina, Mexico and Japan ;

(*b*) the grant by FM to the company of a license to manufacture, process, assemble, use and sell the Licensed products in India under the New Patents and to utilise the Current Technical Information in the possession of the FM as well as New Technical Information in the manufacture, processing, assembly, use and sale of the Licensed Products in India ;

(*c*) the deputation of the competent trained personnel to the premises of the company by FM for the purpose of instructing and assisting the company on all matters relating to the manufacture of Licensed Products, and

(*d*) the training of the company's technical personnel at the FM's manufacturing facilities in USA in connection with the manufacture of the Licensed Products.

The conditions of the License Agreement, if translated into

---

18. Gabriel India Ltd., Prospectus (1978), p. 7.

money, imply an immediate cash benefit to FM by about Rs. 34 lakhs which is nearly equivalent to its cash payment of Rs. 36.96 lakhs to buy 14 per cent shares of the enlarged size of Gabriel India Limited. Firstly, in consideration of the supply by FM to the company of the Current Technical Information the company has agreed to pay Rs. 9 lakhs to the FM. Secondly, for the use by the company of the Current Patent Rights the company has agreed to pay to the FM an additional sum of Rs. 1.8 lakhs. Thirdly, "in consideration of the technical services and assistance to be rendered by the FM to the company both in USA and India, the company has agreed with FM to reimburse them all living and travelling expenses of FM's personnel while on assignments requested by the company and to pay all travel, living expenses and salary of the company's personnel in training in both USA and India or for any other purposes."[19] Training cost of Indian Technicians abroad has been estimated to be Rs. 14.80 lakhs. Fourthly, the company has agreed to buy machines and other equipment worth Rs. 58.95 lakhs from the FM. If profit margin on the value of these imported machines is assumed to be 15 per cent of sales, which is on the lower side for specialised machinery, FM is expected to get a profit of about Rs. 9 lakhs. This is a conservative estimate of the fall out of the License Agreement because there are other beneficiaries in the United States who are supplying machinery worth of Rs. 246.85 lakhs to the company. And quite a few of these beneficiaries might have received these orders from Gabriel at the 'recommendation' of FM or Maremont. In any case, FM would get a cash benefit of Rs. 33.80 lakhs on account of these four considerations.

In addition, the company has agreed to pay to FM a royalty on all Licensed Products sold for use in India during the royalty period at the rate of 5 per cent of the company's net ex-factory selling price and at the rate of 6 per cent of the company's net ex-factory selling price of all License Products sold for export outside India. The royalty period, for the purpose of the License Agreement, shall be the last five years of the License Agreement, even though the company may commence commercial production within the first three years of the date of the License Agreement. This means that the royalty is expected to be paid on the company's full swing production.

---

19. *Ibid.*

How much will be the incidence of the Royalty payment ?
It depends, of course, on the company's annual sales both in
India and abroad. No information is supplied by the company
about the expected sales by its bearings division. However, it is
possible to make an intelligent guess in terms of the sales-networth ratio of Gabriel India Limited over the last five years. The
annual sales of the Gabriel India Limited as a ratio to its
networth have fluctuated from 1.16 in 1974 to 1.87 in 1976,
around a five yearly average of 1.50. Using sales-networth ratio
of 1.5 and networth of bearings division to be Rs. 2.40 crores we
get an estimated annual sales around Rs. 3.60 crores. Therefore,
the royalty payment can be about Rs. 18 lakhs (5 per cent of
Rs. 3.60 crores) per year amounting to a total of Rs. 90 lakhs in
five years.

Thus the collaboration agreement has four important aspects.
First, FM pays Rs. 36.96 lakhs to purchase 14 per cent shares of
the company. Second, the company pays, in return, Rs. 33.80
lakhs to use FM's technical information, patent rights and training facilities. Third, the company pays about Rs. 90 lakhs as
royalty to FM. Fourth, FM will get 14 per cent of the total
dividend of the company in future, which is expected to be more
than Rs. 2 lakhs a year because the current dividend of the
company is Rs. 11.4 lakhs. And above all FM has protected its
market in USA, France, Italy, Spain, Argentina, Mexico and
Japan against Indian exports of bimetal strips and bearings.

Besides, fiscal benefits will accrue to the company under
various schemes of the Government of India and provisions of the
Indian Income Tax Act of 1961. For example, under Sections
80 HH, 80 J, 32 A and host of others. The implications of these
fiscal benefits to the company are quite significant. The bearings
project involves the purchase of plant and machinery worth of
Rs. 413.61 lakhs. Therefore, the company can straight away
write off 25 per cent of this amount, that is Rs. 103.40 lakhs
from taxable profits. Subsequently, 7.5 per cent of the capital
employed (which amounts to Rs. 455.04 lakhs) that is, Rs. 34
lakhs of profits will be tax free for five years. This comes to
Rs. 170 lakhs. And twenty per cent of the profit will be tax
free for ten years, in any case. This will not be less than Rs. 200

lakhs in five years. Thus the company will enjoy complete exemption from the taxation on Rs. 473.4 lakhs of profits (103.4+170+200) at least for the first five years of production. Strangely enough, this amount is more than twice the company's net profit before tax over the last five years, which comes to Rs. 218 lakhs. This means that the company may not have to pay any profit tax to the Government for the next five years as long as its future performance is twice as good as that during the last five years (and during the last five years the foreign shareholders have recovered their initial investment five times over).

The case study of Gabriel suggests a method of estimating the cost of transfer of technology. There is a direct as well as indirect cost of technical collaboration. The direct cost is usually incurred by the use of technical information. It consists of cost of training the workers, payment for the use of patent rights and transfer of blue prints and designs etc., and payments of royalty. The indirect cost is usually borne by the society in the form of fiscal and other incentives and dependence on foreign collaborator for supplies of machinery and spare parts. In the case of Gabriel the direct cost of collaboration in the first year is Rs. 51.80 lakhs (technical fee Rs. 10.8 lakhs, training cost Rs. 14 lakhs, margin on imported machines Rs. 9 lakhs and royalty payment per year Rs. 18 lakhs) and the indirect cost is Rs. 26.35 lakhs. Thus the total cost of collaboration is Rs. 78.15 lakhs against the networth of Bearing project of Rs. 239 lakhs. The Indian companies, however, do not feel the full impact of this heavy cost because a major portion is absorbed by the Government of India, and indirectly by Indian public in the form of 'incentives'.

Same is the case with the *Indian Industry of Dyestuff and Intermediaries* (sample of 13 was taken having the minimum capacity of 500 tonnes per year). The export coefficient was again lowest for Cluster I (0.0970) and highest for Cluster IV (0.3882). The import coefficient was stated to be the highest for Cluster II but again lowest for Clusters III and IV.

RECENT CASES OF TRANSFER OF TECHNOLOGY

1. *Graphite Vicarb India Limited* : The Graphite Vicarb entered into a financial and technical collaboration agreement with Vicarb S.A. of French multinational for the production of impervious graphite equipment. The plant is to be located at Nasik (Maharashtra). The French Co. in turn has purchased 2 lakh equity shares for the value of Rs. 20 lakhs. In consideration thereof the company will provide plant and machinery worth of Rs. 41.9 lakhs.[20] The Indian counterpart, in addition, will import certain grades and sizes of graphite from the parent firm. At the same time other clauses included in the agreement are :

(a) the company will pay Rs. 10 lakhs to the parent firm for imparting technical know-how ;

(b) the company will pay royalty of 3 per cent of net sale price quarterly for a period of five years from the date of commencement of commercial production ;

(c) the company will pay for charges to be incurred on training of Indian personnels at the parent firm.

Besides, all the concessions will be provided under various provisions of the Indian Income Tax Act, 1961 under Sections 32-A, 32(i) (iia), 35-D and 80-I. The direct cost and indirect cost of this technology transfer will be exorbitant similar to that of Gabriel.

2. *Lorcom (Protectives) Limited*[21] : Lorcom is to produce the rubber contraceptives (condoms) with the technical collaboration of LRC Overseas Ltd., a UK multinational. The project is to be located at Chikalthana near Aurangabad, a notified industrially backward district of Maharashtra. Lorcom is to be provided with 3 lakhs equity shares of Rs. 10 each by the LRC worth of Rs. 30 lakhs. The Lorcom, as per the collaboration agreement has to pay for, *inter alia* :

(a) 1,00,000 pound sterling as a technical fees (subject to tax) in lump sum (which at present rate of pound comes

---

20. See Prospectus of the Vicarb India Ltd., 1983, pp. 7-8.
21. Prospectus, 1982, p. 7.

around Rs. 18 lakhs constituting more than half of the value of equity participation).

(*b*) royalty of 3 per cent (subject to tax) of net ex-factory selling price annually in pound sterling for five years from the date of the commencement of commercial production ;

(*c*) additional royalty of 2 per cent (subject to tax) of net ex-factory selling price of the product (exclusive of excise duty) for a period of five years from the date of commencement of commercial production. (This is to be paid in Indian currency).

The company has already remitted 53,332 pound sterling (net of taxes) to the LRC. The Indian company will import from the LRC the plant and machinery worth of Rs. 38 lakhs which will yield to the LRC a sum of Rs. 5.70 lakhs (at the profit margin of 15 per cent).

Thus, the total receipts of the LRC in the first year of its working will offset the equity contribution by it. This company is also subject to all concessions available under the various provisions of the Indian Income Tax Act, 1961 besides a central subsidy of Rs. 15 lakhs for being established in the notified industrially backward area.

IMPACT ON EMPLOYMENT AND HUMAN RESOURCE DEVELOPMENT

It is an undisputed fact that most of the technology trans-ferred by multinational corporations to the developing nations are capital intensive contrary to their needs of labour intensive techniques. Dudley Seers, commissioned by the ILO to study high techonology industry in Columbia, found that whereas it took 45,000 pesos to employ one worker in 1957, by 1966 it took 1,00,000 pesos. A more recent study, by one of the authors, of 257 manufacturing firms throughout Latin America shows that global corporations use less than half the number of employees per $ 10,000 of sales that local firms do. From 1925-

1970 the percentage of the Latin American work force employed in the manufacturing.sector actually decreased.[22]

A Wall Street Journal report on Brazil gives some idea of what these figures mean in human terms.[23]

"Far from such workers (60 cents a day cane harvestors) Brazil's modernisation actually victimises thousands. When a salt company bought new equipments, efficiency soared, but 7,000 people lost their jobs. In Ponce de Carvalhos, many suffer indirectly from the mechanisation of sugar plantations in far-off parts of Brazil. This has made the local plantations uneconomic... A sixty years old woman who had worked twenty years on one plantation says she and 1000 other workers were told to 'harvest your crop, plant grass for cattle, and get out.' She now earns $6.5 a month washing clothes. A 41 years old man who worked 18 years at the Mary-of-Mercy sugar mill now peddles bread by the roadside for 54 cents a day."

The job crisis is a consequence of what James Grant calls the 'artificial cheapening of the price of capital and the artificial increase in the price of labour." Poor countries have encouraged urban oriented factories and large scale mechanised farming as the fastest route to modernisation at a time when the latest machines use less and less labour. Poor countries subsidise foreign capital by inflating interest rates, by making generous tax concession, legal and illegal and because of their inability to control transfer prices. At the same time, the modest improvement in minimum wage laws, fringe benefits, and union bargaining power mean higher labour costs for global corporations, which often pay more than the traditional sectors of the economy. Thus global corporations have every incentive to buy more machines and to employ fewer worker. The multinational corporations are thus responsible for disorganising the domestic labour market and the existing imperfections have been further intensified by these

22. The study of 257 manufacturing firms in Latin America can be found in Muller and Morgenstern, KYKLOS, April 1974 and Trimestre Economico, Jan./April 1974, "The Multinational Corporations and the Underdevelopment of the Third World." See also Streeton and Lall, whose 8 country Study also confirms these employment effects, quoted in 'Global Reach,' Barnet. Richard J. and Muller, Ronald E., 1974, p. 169.
23. Report published in series of two parts, the Wall Street Journal on April 14 and 21, 1972, p. 1.

giants. The same arguments have been advanced by Horst (1971, 1973) and Steevans (1974) and an empirical study in this support provided by Horst (1973).

CONCLUSION

Technology is the key to economic power in the modern world. Global corporations, as we have seen, are for the most part oligopolies. Their enviable position usually rests on some piece of exclusive technology which they are not anxious to make available to actual or potential competitors. At the same time if they are to operate globally they are forced to spread their technology. But the poor countries are likely to get processes which are abandoned elsewhere or on the verge of abandonment. Distributing the last generation's technology to poor countries is a good way to prolong its profitable life. Thus in many cases the imported technology is too expensive and too complicated. Having been developed for the needs of industrialised societies, it does not solve and rather aggravate the problems in poor countries.

There is no doubt that the imported technology has had a major impact on poor countries, but not the positive effects as hoped and claimed. Of course, there are certain studies[24] which have been devoted to their positive effects but again the imperialistic bias of such studies could not be ruled out. There is no doubt that the interests of technology suppliers and the recipients do aften clash in one way or the other.

There are some economists (Ford 1971, Freeman 1971 and others) who consider the multinational corporations as 'paragon of all virtues' disparage such criticism as expression of irrational nationalism or a wasteful vanity. However, the attempt to prevent foreign control of technology is in fact quite rational. It is plausible that the assumed efficiency of the manufacturing units closely associated with the multinational corporations may be the result of their operation in an oligopolistic/monopolistic market structure that prevails in the protected domestic market. It is in this context that one has to interpret the oft-repeated

24. Koizumi, Tetsunori and Kopecky, Kenneth J., "Foreign Direct Investment, Technology Transfer and Domestic Employment Effect," Journal of International Economics (10) 1980, pp. 1-20.

argument that foreign collaboration in the process of import substitution may lead to negative trade impact but does not prelude great possibility of income generation. In a sense, therefore, it is the institutional structure in the developing countries that makes the multinationals appear most efficient rather than its built in characteristics.[25]

SUGGESTIONS

1. There should be an independent national agency to screen and review the technology which is proposed to be transferred from the multinationals. This body should be manned by the technocrats. Every technology transfer proposal must be approved by this agency. This will help in making the appropriate technology available to the host countries. While allowing such technology transfer not only economic but social implications should also be given due consideration.

2. The firm selling/transferring technology to the developing countries should be asked, on a mandatory basis, to establish R and D facilities in the host countries. This will provide for host country's participation in R and D activities. Only those products should be allowed to produce which are needed in conformity with domestic environment.

3. All the technical collaboration agreements must be viewed keeping in mind the various restrictive clauses, over pricing (at the international standard) and the clauses making a recurring liability (like payment of royalties, etc.) on the domestic firms and on the foreign exchange resources of the recipient country.

4. At the same time all academic institutions and the researches going on in these institutions must have vocational relationship with the industry and trade. This will give better oppor- tunities to domestic potential of the scientific personnel and commercial uses thereof. Most of the technical researches are still to reach the stage of industrial application in developing countries in general and India in particular. This will not only help in checking the 'brain drain' but will also boost the development in the country.

25. Subrahmanmain, K.K. and Pillai, P. Mohan, "Multinationals and Indian Exports," Allied Publishers, New Delhi, 1979.

TRANSFER PRICING AND RESTRICTIVE BUSINESS PRACTICES AND MULTINATIONAL CORPORATIONS

Introduction

Transfer Pricing

Concept of Transfer Pricing

Underlying Considerations for Transfer Pricing :
  (a) Maximising Present Profits
  (b) Minimising Risk and Uncertainty

Effects of Transfer Pricing

Cases Relating to Transfer Pricing

Difficulties in Investigating the Transfer Pricing Problem

Conclusions ; Suggestions

Restrictive Business Practices of MNCs

Functional Classification of Restrictive Business Practices

Restrictive Business Practices by the MNCs in India

Development Implications of Restrictive Business Practices

   Rural Development

   Natural Resource Development

   Output

   Employment

   Income Distribution

   Resource Allocation

Conclusions

4

Transfer Pricing* and Restrictive Business Practices and MNCs

INTRODUCTION

One of the most important dimensions of the operations of multinational corporations is their frequent recourse to the transfer pricing mechanism for their intracorporate transactions and various restrictive clauses attached to their collaboration agreements—financial or technical.

Both these practices have resulted not only in loss of revenue through evasion of tax, foreign exchange losses by over-invoicing and under-invoicing devices but also resulted in narrowing down the size of the markets which are otherwise available to the manufacturers. Various restrictive clauses have been attached with collaboration agreements ranging from export restrictions to certain markets to total ban on sales to some other areas. Even the clauses of prior permission were added to such agreements before exporting to or entering into some agreement with other countries or buyers by host countries' affiliates or subsidiaries. Consequent upon this the host countries have suffered a loss in terms of utilisation of their resources on the one hand and working as captive units for parent organisations on the other, resulting in dependence for know-how. This dependence has given rise to various political overtones, which are sometimes so subtle that are not easy to visualise in the short period. The argument of resources inflow has also been belied by empirical evidences particularly in the case of developing countries.

*Published in the Economic Times, Bombay, October 21, 22, 1985.

67

TRANSFER PRICING

One of the practices of the Multinational Corporations, which is of particular concern to the countries in which they operate, is the fixing of prices of their goods and services traded between the Corporations and their affiliates located in different countries. Intra-corporate transfer pricing by a multi-regional company within a country may matter little to the national government as all the benefits are retained within the country itself. But intra-firm trading by the multinational corporation has serious implications on the economy of host developing countries.

In the manufacturing sector the problem of transfer pricing has remained a curious blind spot in the rapidly growing academic literature on the multinational corporations and its effects on trade and development. Two major studies on the balance of payment effect of overseas investment on the capital-exporting countries, Hufbauer and Adler (1968) on the US, and Reddaway (1967) on the UK, have not even recognised the problem, while a great deal of theoretical discussion of multinational corporations, for example, Kindelberger (1969) and (1970), or Johnson (1969) have barely noted the existence of intra-firm trade (a major exception is Vaitsos, 1974)—the implication being either that such trade is very similar in its economic effects to inter-firm trade (between unrelated parties), or that it is quantitatively insignificant. Even some of the economists who have recognised that intra-firm trade creates problems (Dunning 1972) ; (Vernon 1971) ; (Brooke and Remmers 1970) seem to have underestimated its full extent.

CONCEPT OF TRANFER PRICING

Transfer princing may be defined as the "pricing of transactions, both of commodities and intangibles, such as technological services and brand names between different branches of a multinational corporation."[1] It can, therefore, be termed as a clearing price entered in the books for transactions within a firm—the firm in this context meaning the entire business enterprise con-

---

1. Lall, Sanjay, 'Transfer Pricing and Multinational Corporations', Monthly Review, December 1974, p. 36.

sidered as a unit.[2] The transfer pricing[3] may be symbolically expressed as

$Pc—Pw/Pw \times 100$

Where Pc is price actually paid in a country under study

Where Pw is comparable world market price.

Thus the transfer pricing refers not only to (a) transfer of goods from one part of the firm to another, but also to (b) transfer of patents or rights to use patent processes against payment of royalties, and (c) supply of technical services by one part of the firm to another part compensated by service fees or managerial fees. Determination of prices in intra-firm trade takes place according to considerations different from those in inter-firm trade. More so, the intra-firm trade is not an insignificant proportion of trade by the multinational corporation and it gives rise to so many serious issues relating to the effects on trade, welfare and national control. Certain policy implications are also not ruled out.

The fact that a transaction involving a transfer or sale of goods takes place within a firm, regardless of whether or not the firm spans different countries, and the firm is free within broad limits to assign whatever price it likes to those goods, means that the traditional theory of pricing in competitive, oligopolistic or monopolistic markets ceases to apply to the process of transfer pricing. The essential difference is simply that in transactions of the open market or between unrelated parties, the buyers and sellers are trying to maximise their profits at 'each others expense', while in an intra-firm transaction the price is merely an accounting device and the two parties are trying to maximise 'joint profits.' It is possible that the accounting price may approximate the arm's length price of the goods but certainly there is no presumption that this should be so ; any other price is equally plausible. Any discussion of transfer pricing problem has to

---

2. UN Document ST/ESA/18, 'Tax Treaties between Developed and Developing Countries', New York, 1975, Fifth Report, p. 63.
3. Though this formula is generally expressed in terms of over-pricing but transfer pricing has been generally found in the form of overpricing in the host developing nations. Thus the overpricing and transfer pricing has been used interchangeably for the sake of simplicity.

assume that there exists a yardstick by which the effects of the price can be measured ; there must, in other words, be an arm's length price, and the goods may be 'overpriced' if transfer pricing is higher, and 'underpriced' if transfer pricing is lower than this price. It is not necessary for there to be an open market price ; from the firm's point of view all that is required is that it should know at what price it would be prepared to sell to unrelated concerns. When a good is overpriced, the firm transfers funds, *via* the pricing channel, from the buying to the selling firms ; declared profits are thus understated and overstated respectively in comparison with the situation where no intra-firm transactions take place. The reverse happens with underpricing.

UNDERLYING CONSIDERATIONS FOR TRANSFER PRICING

Various considerations are made for opting the transfer pricing mechanism by the multinational corporations. These may be :—

   (*a*) to save tax

   (*b*) to get round any ceiling on profit remittances

   (*c*) to reduce the corporations' liability in the country where currency is weakening

   (*d*) to beat down the union demand for higher wages and so on.

But the objectives of transfer pricing may be grouped under two broad headings : those which maximise the present value of MNCs' profits, and those which minimise present and future risk about the value of profits.[4]

(*a*) MAXIMISING PRESENT PROFITS

Bearing in mind that the multinational corporations are concerned to maximise the value of profits of all their operations taken together, and abstracting for the moment from the problems of risk minimisation, a number of conditions can be postulated in which transfer pricing will be used.

---

4. Lall, Sanjay, 'The Multinational Corporations', Macmillan, 1980, p. 112.

(*i*) *Loss in One Centre of Operations*—When the MNC makes losses in one of the countries it operates in, it would be induced to remit profits to that country so as to minimise its overall tax burden. Vaitsos (1974) has tried to construct a theory of transfer pricing[5] on the grounds that multinational corporations make losses in their home country (in our example country *A*) because of heavy overhead and research expenses there. Thus the loss incurring unit will overprice its exports to the unit (branch and/or affiliate) running on profits. S. Lall[6] considers this argument of limited applicability on the ground that carry forward of losses are allowed by some countries not beyond a certain period. But this argument holds water for the reason that the loss incurring unit enjoys the maximum period to offset the tax liability and by the time the unit stabilises it explores another channels for transfer pricing. In India most of the foreign collaborations are taking the advantage of this because transfer pricing is simply an accounting adjustment which these MNCs do with utmost adroitness. Moreover, the multiplicity of ways of tax concessions provide ample avenues for tax avoidance which results in overall tax losses to the host country.

(*ii*) *Taxes, Tariffs and subsidies*—One of the best considerations for the use of transfer pricing is international differences in tax and tariff rates.[7] Export subsidies may also be introduced as a factor affecting such calculation. If tax rates are higher in *B* than *A*, and the parent MNC supplies imports to the subsidiary, it would pay the firm to overprice these transactions and move profits to *A* as long as the difference in effective tax rates exceeds the tariff in *B* on those imports. If tariff rates are higher, it would pay to underprice the imports. Similarly, if the subsidiary is exporting to the parent it would pay to underprice the transactions as long as the tax rate differential plus the saving in import duty in *A* exceeded the export subsidy in *B*. If trade is taking place in both directions, the MNC may underprice imports into *B*

5. Vaitsos, C.V., 'Inter Country Income Distribution and Transnational Corporations', Oxford, Clarendon Press, 1974.
6. *Ibid.*, S. Lall, p. 113.
7. Horst, T., 'The Theory of the Multinational Firm : Optimal Behaviour under Different Tariff and Tax Rates', Journal of Political Economy, Vol. 79, 1971. Copithorne, L.W., 'International Corporate Transfer Prices and Government Policy', Canadian Journal of Economics, Vol. IV, 1971. ; Tugendhat, C., 'The Multinational Eyre and Spottiswoode, London, 1971.

to avoid duties and underprice its exports to A to take advantage of exports subsidies in B and lower taxes in A. The extent to which profits can be moved around freely depends on the volume of intra-firm trade, the structure of the firm and the vigilance of the relevant authorities.

(*iii*) *Multiple Exchange Rates*—In some countries which have multiple exchange rates (for instance Columbia before 1966) the rate applicable to capital or intermediate goods' imports, effectively imposing an additional tax on declared profit remittances.

(*iv*) *Quantitative Restrictions*—Limits imposed on the remittances of profits serve a very strong consideration to use the transfer pricing mechanism, especially when other channels such as royalties and management and technical fees to the parent firm, are also controlled. If the subsidiary is exceptionally profitable, and the MNC does not wish to re-invest the profits in B, it may remit them by overpricing imports into B regardless of the extra tariff cost, since any gain in profits abroad would be a net benefit. Furthermore, if the amount of permissible dividends were calculated as a percentage of the MNC's net worth, the firm would be induced to overprice its initial equity contribution which took the form of capital equipment to inflate the capital base.

(*v*) *Existence of Local Shareholders*—The existence of local shareholders in the subsidiary in B may induce the MNC to overprice its imports into B for three reasons. First, to increase its own share of total profits at the cost of local shareholders; Second, to inflate the initial value of capital equipment contributed by way of equity participation; and Third, to act in collusion with the local partners in order to provide funds for accumulation abroad or for resale in the black market.

(*vi*) *Exchange Rate Speculation*—If the exchange rate of either A or B is expected to change and the MNC cannot or will not speculate openly, it may use transfer price to reinforce the normal leads and lags which minimises its obligations in the devaluing currency. The profitability of such speculation would depend on the amount of devaluation expected and the cost of using transfer prices in terms of additional taxes and tariffs.

There is a distinction to be drawn between active speculation for gain, which is basically short term and liable to be reversed after the rates have been re-adjusted (or the crisis escaped), and long term hedging against a basically weak currency. The former is likely to be used by the MNCs in developed countries in periods of exchange crises, while the latter is likely to occur in developing countries, particularly those ridden with higher rate of inflation.[8]

(b) MINIMISING RISK AND UNCERTAINTY

The long term profitability of a MNC is subject to various pressures in the different areas it operates in, and the judicious use of transfer pricing to show low levels of profits may well contribute to insure its future existence and stability. Moreover, the transfer pricing is done deliberately to show low level of profitability to keep all possible criticism at bay.

(i) *Balance of Payment and Exchange Rate Pressures*—Some countries may be deemed as risk countries because of the threat of impending restrictions on remittances, periodic devaluations and the like, and the MNC may adopt a long term strategy of moving profits out *via* transfer pricing.

(ii) *Political and Social Pressures*—These may range from trade union pressures for a larger share of profits to the government threats to nationalisation because of exploitation. In fact, any host country which tries to control or limit the activities of the MNCs may be considered a more or less undesirable are to declare high profits in, and for long term safety, regardless of tax tariff or other short term factors, the transfer pricing mechanism may be used to remit profits abroad. Expectations of the individual firms are likely to differ considerably as far as this is concerned, however, and the built-in deterrent that the discovery of such a policy would itself exacerbate the situation and may induce firms not to over-indulge. Nevertheless, the environment of a particular host country in the eyes of the multinational cor-

---

8. Brooke, M.Z. and Remmers, H.L., 'The Strategy of Multinational Enterprise', Longman, London, 1970.
   Brooke, M.Z. and Remmers, H.L., 'The Multinational Company in Europe', Longman, London, 1972.

porations may well be one of the most important factors influenc-
ing the long-term use of the transfer pricing channel ; the inbuilt
secrecy is ideal in situations where there are long-term threats to
its operations arising from its profitability.

(*iii*) *Direct Threats to Profits*--The declaration of high profits
may cause a number of reactions which directly reduce the
multinational corporation's profitability. First, the government
may, where appropriate, lower the level of protection on the
firms' final output. If the level of protection is determined by
the government on the basis of the firms' cost of production plus
some reasonable allowance of profit, the multinational corporation
can easily raise the protection and its profits, by inflating its cost
by over-pricing intra-firm imports. The existence of such an
instrument in the hands of the MNCs gives it a strong weapon
when bargaining for concessions with the host governments,
one which they may not even be aware of. Second, a similar case
arises when governments impose price controls (as is very
commonly found in India and that too in pharmaceutical industry
in particular) on products of the MNCs the level at which
prices are fixed being determined again by the cost of production.
This happens most often when protection is granted by the
banning of imports rather than by tariffs, and domestic prices
are sought to be kept in check by direct means. There is
evidence that over-pricing of imports has been caused by this
factor in India and Columbia. Third, the danger of increased
competition from other MNCs or local manufacturers, (may be
attracted by high declared profits) may also cause transfer
pricing to be used in exceptionally profitable countries.[9] The
threat of nationalisation or a gradual process of nationalisation
would be speeded up by these high profits and the government, as
a part of its efforts, may raise the level of taxation or imposing
special levies on them.

Though it is not necessary that the mechanism of transfer
pricing would always be used to the detriment of one country

9. Vaitsos, C.V., 'Inter Country Income Distribution and Transnational
Corporations', Oxford, Clarendon Press, 1974.

(developed or developing countries) but "the cards are in fact stacked heavily against the less developed countries."[10] Greater the degree of control over the activities of MNC greater will be the possibility of using the transfer pricing mechanism.[11]

EFFECTS OF TRANSFER PRICING

It is a fact that practice of transfer pricing is generally harmful to the host country. These harmful effects may be grouped as :

(*i*) loss of legitimate tax revenue,

(*ii*) loss of higher export earning,

(*iii*) loss of profit in regard to the income of local shareholders,

(*iv*) hastening devaluations of currency in case of continuing adverse balance of payment,

(*v*) stifling the open competitions by declaring low profits and keeping the potential competitors at bay.

(*vi*) monopolising the production, marketing and distribution of products.

CASES RELATING TO THE TRANSFER PRICING

There are many cases of over-pricing in every industry supporting the world wide practice of transfer pricing. The transfer pricing may be ascertained from two general evidences—one in cross comparison of the same commodities sold at different prices at different places, two, by investigating real rate of profit which is not generally shown in the balance sheets of the multinational corporations.

The extent of over-pricing is different in different industries, which is ranging from ten per cent to ten thousand per cent. Several instances of over-pricing have been documented in Columbia, where subsidiaries in the pharmaceutical industry paid 155 per cent more than c.i.f. price for intermediate drugs imported

---

10. Lall, Sanjay, 'The Multinational Corporations', Macmillan, London, 1980, p. 116.

11. Lack of freedom of subsidiaries in determining transfer pricing is noted in a Ph.D. Thesis by J. Shulman, quoted by Tugendhat (1971), Chapter 10.

from parent firms. Over-pricing of 40 per cent was also found in the rubber industry, 26 per cent in chemical industry and 16-60 per cent in electronics industry.[12] The pharmaceutical industry is subject to excessive overpricing. An examination of 72 cases in Iran for the late 1960s shows, for instance, that 38 per cent of the cases had over-pricing of intermediate drug chemicals of upto 199 per cent, another 50 per cent of the cases from 200 per cent to 999 per cent and 6 per cent cases of even higher magnitude. In one case the imported chemical (doxycycline) was over-priced by more than 10,000 per cent. In Egypt an instance of overpricing of 159 per cent is reported for 1965. Many instances of over-pricing have been found in Pakistan, India, Brazil and Turkey.[13]

An example of overpricing of certain raw materials in drug industry may be seen from the Table 4.1 for the period 1970-73.

Table 4 1
Over-pricing of Certain Raw Materials in Drug Industry

Raw Materials	Per Unit Price paid by domestic firms	Per Unit Price paid by firms with MNCs connections	Extent of over-pricing (%)
Paranitrolune	0.0375	0.0537	143
Sodium Nitrate	0.0116	0.0380	328
Dibitrochlorobenze	0.0185	0.0321	173
Orthotoludine	0.0531	0.1321	249
Bromine	0.0876	0.1086	124
Parahitrolune	0.0375	0.1018	271

Quoted by Som Deo, Multinational Corporations ; The Exploiting Feuds-II, Economic Affairs, April-June, 1980.

Here the Columbian case has been selected as a case study. The reason is that this case was supported even by the governmental investigations. Though the information relating to the

12. Deo, Som, "The Multinational Corporations and the Developing Countries," Economic Affairs, Vol. 20, No. 8. August 1975. Calcutta, p. 347.
13. Deo, Som, "Modus Operandi of Drug Multinationals." Economic Affairs, Vol. 22, No. 4, April 1977, p. 141.

transfer pricing is highly scarce in any country where the MNCs operate.

After the Columbian government passed the Decree 444 in 1967 imposing controls relating to foreign exchange, flows of exchange by the foreign investors, an investigation of transfer pricing mechanism was undertaken with the assumption that the ramifications of transfer pricing were far greater than dividends and royalties. The main sector was pharmaceuticals (being the dominantly owned by foreign firms), the rubber, chemicals and electrical industry were also investigated, though much less intensively. The research carried out for 1968 by the Planning Office (Planeacion) and for 1967-70 by the Import Control Board (INCOMEX) by employing qualified chemists and technicians and compared the prices actually charged on imports with prices paid for comparable commodities by locally owned firms, by other Latin American countries, and in world market generally.

In arriving at the world prices average of available quotations rather than the lowest ones were taken and at the same time allowed for transportation cost and 20 per cent margin of error. Planeacion discovered a weighted average of over-pricing by 155 per cent (for 1968) and INCOMEX of 87 per cent (for 1969-70). The savings achieved by the government action came to US $ 3 3 million annually in the pharmaceutical sector alone, out of a total bill of $ 15 million.

Rubber imports were found to be over-priced by 44 per cent, chemical inputs by 25 per cent and electrical components by 54 per cent. Studies on transfer pricing in other countries especially Chile, showed that pattern was almost similar.[14]

While investigating the problem (conducted by the UNCTAD) Sanjay Lall took the sample of 14 foreign companies in Columbia. The study also used the evidences uncovered by planeacion and INCOMEX and combining it with the balance sheet figures for these firms, the effect of over-pricing can be seen from the Table 4.2. The figures are related to the period prior to the legal action taken by government. It covers 11 pharmaceutical, 1 rubber and

---

14. UNCTAD, 1971.

2 electrical firms. Among these 12 were wholly foreign owned (marked *A*) and 2 foreign majority owned firms (marked *B*).

Column 2 of the Table suggests that the weighted average of over-pricing ranged from 33 per cent to over 300 per cent for the imports of pharmaceutical sector, from 24 per cent to 81 per cent in other sectors. The difference made to profitability from proved over-pricing (column 4) ranges from 2 to 112 per cent of net worth in the former and from 0.3 to 6 per cent in the latter. Such profits

Over-pricing by and Profitability of 14 Foreign Firms in Columbia (1966-70)

Industries and firms	1	2	3	4	5	6
Pharmaceuticals						
1. (A)	52.1	158.3	7.6	41.5	79.6	87.2
2. (B)	20.1	39.5	11.2	2 0	10.0	21.2
3. (A)	100.0	56.6	16.5	19.6	19.6	36.1
4. (A)	28.1	81.0	6.3	5.6	19.9	26.2
5. (A)	32.4	288.9	6.3	19.2	59.3	65.6
6. (A)	39.1	33.5	0.1	2.5	63.9	64.0
7. (A)	35.2	33.7	12.4	3.1	8.8	21.2
8. (A)	54.1	95.4	—7.4	17.9	33.1	26.1
9. (A)	48.6	83.7	42.8	111.7	229.8	272.6
10. (A)	44 2	313.8	27.5	39.6	89.6	117.1
11. (A)	30.9	138.9	5.9	9.9	32.0	37.9
Rubber						
12. (B)	60.0	40.0	8.3	6.1	10.2	18.5
Electrical						
13. (A)	22.3	24 1	8.1	0.3	1.3	9.4
14. (A)	30.4	81.1	0.7	1.8	5.9	6.6

Columns : No. 1. % Imports investigated
No. 2. % proved over-pricing
No. 3. Declared profits as % of Net Worth
No. 4. Profits on proved over-pricing as % of Net Worth.
No. 5. Profits on over-pricing total imports % Net Worth
No. 6. Co. (3+5).

Notes : (1) (A) wholly owned foreign firms
(2) (B) foreign owned 51-99%
(3) based on over-price defined as
Pc—Pw/Pw×100

exceed the value of declared profit for 9 out of 14 firms. If we impute the proved level of over-pricing to total imports of the firms including the imports not investigated, we find that profits on over-pricing rise substantially in pharmaceuticals, but not so dramatically in the other industries. Imputed over-pricing profits exceed declared profits for 11 of the 14 firms (Table 4.2).

Different foreign firms have different attitude to transfer pricing in Columbia because, there are quantitative limits on profit remittances as well as price controls on pharmaceutical and rubber products, duties on imports of intermediate products are quite low, especially in pharmaceuticals, there is considerable suspicion of foreign enterprises and restriction on their activities, and some of the foreign firms are exceptionally profitable. Many other developing countries are in similar situations.

DIFFICULTIES IN INVESTIGATING THE TRANSFER PRICING PROBLEM

The problem of transfer pricing is political as well as economic. Political in the sense that a fiscal policy and transfer pricing is taken to show a liberal and welcoming attitude to foreign investment and change to a strict policy may be taken a hostile switch. In part, however, the problem is practical. There are enormous difficulties faced by host countries wishing to investigate transfer pricing by large, monopolistic, multiproduct transnationals. These difficulties arise from three different factors, *viz.,*

(a) an uneven incidence of transfer pricing across different industries and by different firms,

(b) internal and external problems in collecting the data relevant to checking intra-firm pricing, and

(c) conceptual issues in defining correct transfer prices.

CONCLUSIONS

(a) that the trade on the basis of transfer pricing today accounts for a substantial part of the world trade, and will account for a larger proportion in the future if the multinational corporations continue to grow.

(*b*) that the declared earnings of the MNCs are very much smaller than the value of intra-firm trade, so that a relatively minor change in transfer prices can cause a very large change in MNCs profitability, and

(*c*) that the available evidence indicates that transfer pricing is deliberately used to transfer profits from less desirable to more desirable areas, and the existing inbuilt constraints to its use are ineffective.

SUGGESTIONS

Transfer pricing mechanism of the MNCs is highly complex and thus difficult to check. But still some suggestions can be ventured here.

1. The government should try to break the link between imports and parent companies by channeling all imports through an independent State agency or forcing firms to buy elsewhere. But this requires a large administrative commitment.

2. The tax authority should try to judge profits of the MNCs on evidence other than declared profits, say, by their profitability abroad, or their sales, or some such measures. But this may become extremely arbitrary, contentious and liable to corruption. But this has to be done.

3. The government may decide to check transfer prices directly and compare them with the world prices. This may seem difficult but the international indices may be used for the purpose. The dispute may arise only in the case of items when they are not openly traded in the world markets. Here the use of consultants or international agencies may be of great help.

4. All the host governments may get together and tax them jointly, rendering the whole process of profit transfer irrelevant. This may be the most ideal solution.

5. The government may encourage internal checks to the use of transfer pricing by enlarging the share of local equity in the multinational corporations.

6. There should be direct official checks and its effectiveness can be increased by inter-government co-operation and exchange of information (as in the Andean pact countries).

RESTRICTIVE BUSINESS PRACTICES OF THE MNCs

Section 2 (0) of the MRTP Act 1969 defines restrictive trade practices as "a trade practice which has, or may have, the effect of preventing, distorting or restricting competition in any manner and in particular :

(*a*) Which tends to obstruct the flow of capital or resources into the stream of production, or

(*b*) which tends to bring about manipulation of prices, or conditions of delivery or to affect the flow of supplies in the market relating to goods or services in such a manner as to impose on the consumers unjustified costs or restrictions."

Though the above definition has its own implications but certain practices, may be called as 'unfair trade practices' should also be curbed and brought under the umbrella of the MRTP Act. These practices may be like, misleading advertisement and false representations ; bargain sales ; bait and switch selling ; offering of gifts or prizes with intention of not providing them ; conducting promotional contests ; supplying goods that do not comply with safety standards ; hoarding and destruction of goods ; resale price maintenance ; allocational arrangements of markets, etc, etc.

FUNCTIONAL CLASSIFICATION OF RESTRICTIVE BUSINESS PRACTICES

Restrictive business practices in developing countries can be classified into the following areas :

(*a*) Aspects of pricing policies

(*b*) Territorial market and product allocation arrangements (may be classified broadly under export restrictions).

(*c*) Forms of boycott and enforcement measures.

Pricing policies and territorial market and product allocation arrangements are often important elements of the corporate strategies of the MNCs.[15] These elements are closely related to the long term strategies of maximising profits, market growth and stability, among other things, globally. Boycotts and other measures are practices that may be adopted by dominant firms either singly or collusively, to ensure that agreements are complied with as well as to keep competitors out of particular markets. Also strategies involving their use may be defensive or predatory.

Following categories have been identified by the UN study[16] as restrictive business practices :

—Practices relating to exports

—Practices on the levels of production and type of productive activities.

—Practices on the purchases of capital equipments and inputs used in productive activities by subsidiary and affiliates of the multinational corporations.

—Practices relating to the use of industrial property rights as well as know-how.

—Practices in which the firm outside the corporation will act as distributor for their product including (a) regulations concerning the purchase of products other than those that are the principal object of the arrangements, (b) restrictions on handling or manufacturing competing products, (c) restrictions on types of customers to use imported products, and (d) refusal to sell or supply products to other firms.

—Practices relating to territorial and product allocation arrangements.

—Practices relating to expansion and diversification of activities nationally or internationally.

15. UNCTAD, 'The Role of Transnational Corporations in the Trade, in the Manufactures and Semi-manufactures of Developing Countries', Geneva, 1975.

16. UNCTAD, 'Role of Transnational Corporations', p. 6.

—Practices affecting competitors and partners in particular markets.

—Practices relating to the pricing policies like (*a*) fixing prices for inter-corporate transactions, (*b*) fixing prices to be charged for arms-length purchases, including the fixation of sale and resale price for products imported or exported.

An expert group of the United Nations has added more contents to the restrictive business practices by the MNCs in less developing countries,[17] under the following three broad heads :

(*a*) International and national external trade cartels restrictive business practices (RBPs)

agreements fixing prices as to exports and imports ;

collusive tendering ;

market or customer allocational arrangements ;

allocation of quota as to sales and production ;

collective action to enforce arrangements.

(*b*) Domestic Restrictive Business Practices :

price fixing and rebate cartels, collusive tendering, resale price maintenance and other collusive arrangements ;

collective boycotts ;

denial of access to an association joint arrangements or facility that is crucial to competition.

(*c*) RBPs relating to acquisition or abuse of dominant position :

anti-competitive exclusive dealing and anti-competitive refusals to deal ;

unnecessary tied sale or purchases ;

predatory or discriminatory pricing ;

anti-competitive mergers, takeovers or other acquisitions.

---

17. Report of the Second Ad-hoc Group of Experts on 'Restrictive Business Practices', TD/B/C. 2.5/Dev. (1975), pp. 15-16.

Professor Fine has also identified a number of practices in international trade that point to pricing, product and market allocation arrangements as the overpricing considerations.[18]

RESTRICTIVE BUSINESS PRACTICES BY THE MNCs IN INDIA

India, like other developing countries too has been subject to many restrictive business practices (RBPs) by multinational corporations. As has been made clear earlier that India has been subject to mainly two types of RBPs, namely, export restrictions and the restrictions in terms of tied purchases, royalty and sale procedures. In case of other developing countries also the export restrictions have been used most commonly.

RESTRICTIVE CLAUSES IN THE AGREEMENTS

The special clauses in agreements related to exports, sources of supply, production capacity, pattern of production, mode of distribution, sales procedures, minimum royalty rates, etc. Of the 1098 effective agreements in respect of private sector companies, 654 or nearly three-fifts had such clauses. This compares with the position in 1960-64, when 50 per cent of total agreements had regulatory clauses. The increase in such special clauses in agreements was mainly in respect of minority and pure technical companies where the proportions went up from 56 per cent to 65 per cent and from 46 per cent to 60 per cent respectively. By type of clauses, the rise was marked in respect of exports clauses (from 455 in 1963-64 to 956 in 1969-70), and was evident in all three groups of companies, particularly minority companies (from 230 to 457) and pure technical companies (from 169 to 419). The rise in the number of special clauses in respect of other items mentioned above (from 295 to 329) was seen only in the case of minority companies (from 104 to 161) while there was actually a fall in the number of such clauses in agreements for the pure technical companies (from 167 to 144).

Of the total 1,285 special clauses, nearly three-fourths (956) related to export restrictions (Table 4.3). While clauses regarding

---

18. Fine, R., "The Control of Restrictive Business Practices in International Trade ; A viable proposal for an international organisation", International Lawyer 7, No. 3, p. 638.

conditional payments of royalties etc. were 94. These included conditions relating to a fixed minimum payment per year, payment on achieving a given production target, those dependent on compulsory exports, etc. Other special clauses numbered 235, stipulating sources of supply of raw materials, limits on production capacity, manufacture of products similar to collaboration products, arrangements for sales in the domestic market only through collaborator's distributors etc. It was seen that the number of clauses with restrictions on sources of supply of equipment and materials was larger (28) in the case of pure technical companies and also in the case of minority companies (21) but negligible (3) in the case of subsidiaries. The proportion of agreements with such restrictions in the PTC group was also higher (10.5 per cent) than that for minority companies (6.6 per cent) and subsidiaries (4.4 per cent). This may be because in the case of the former it is not possible to have supplies tied to equity participation as in the case of the latter two groups. There were special clauses relating to export in the case of all the three categories of foreign collaboration companies, namely, subsidiaries (77 per cent), minority and pure technical companies (74 per cent each). The clauses relating to conditions imposed on the nature and mode of payments formed 7 per cent while other regulatory

Table 4.3
Classification of Regulatory Clauses (1964-70)

Types of Regulatory Clauses	Subsi-diaries	Minority Companies	Pure technical companies	Total
1. Export clauses	80	457	419	956
2. Conditional payment clauses	5	48	41	94
3. Other Restrictions	19	113	103	235
4. Total (1 to 3)	104	618	563	1,285
A. Total number of agreements with regulatory clauses	68	320	266	654
B. Total number of agreements	167	489	442	1,098
C. A as percentage of B	40.7	65.4	60.2	59.6

Source : Foreign collaboration in Indian Industry, Second Survey Report, 1974, RBI, p. 102.

Table 4.4

Country-wise Classification of Agreements with Export Restrictions (1964-70)

Country	Subsidiaries		Minority companies		Pure Technical Companies		Total	
	Number of Agreements		Number of Agreement		Number of Agreements		Number of Agreement	
	With export restrictions	Total	With export restrictions	Total	With export restrictions	Total	With export restrictions	Total
U.K.	26	85	101	170	67	127	194	382
U.S.A.	12	33	62	106	43	74	117	213
West Germany	10	11	48	75	40	74	98	160
Switzerland	5	14	14	30	19	42	38	86
Japan	—	4	7	22	9	36	16	62
France	—	—	9	20	14	19	23	39
Italy	—	—	9	18	5	8	14	26
Canada	—	4	2	5	1	2	3	11
Netherlands	—	—	5	16	3	4	8	20
Sweden	—	6	7	10	3	6	10	22
East European countries	—	—	—	—	8	19	8	19
Others	8	10	7	17	20	31	35	58
Total	61	167	271	489	232	442	564	1,098

Source : Foreign Collaboration in Indian Industry, Second Survey Report 1974, RBI, p. 103.

Table 4.5
Industry-wise Classification of Agreements with Export Restriction (1964-70)

Industry	Subsidiaries Number of Agreements With export restrictions	Subsidiaries Number of Agreements Total	Minority Companies Number of Agreements With export restrictions	Minority Companies Number of Agreements Total	Pure Technical Companies Number of Agreements With export restrictions	Pure Technical Companies Number of Agreements Total	Total Number of Agreements With export restrictions	Total Number of Agreements Total
I. Plantations and Mining	1	1	3	7	—	—	4	8
II. Petroleum	—	3	—	—	—	—	—	3
III. Manufacturing	60	155	258	460	230	435	548	1,050
Foods, beverages and tobacco	—	2	1	2	2	2	3	6
Textile products	—	2	—	14	6	35	6	51
Transport equipment	4	7	49	73	28	42	81	122
Machinery and machine tools	8	23	89	112	87	128	184	263
Metals & metal products	18	27	15	37	27	59	60	123
Electrical goods and machinery	23	34	55	93	48	82	126	209
Chemical & allied products	5	45	32	84	18	51	55	180
(i) Basic industrial	2	19	21	47	6	12	29	78
(ii) Medicines and Pharmaceuticals	2	21	10	19	7	20	19	60
(iii) Others	1	5	1	18	5	19	7	42
Rubber goods	1	5	1	7	4	7	6	19
Miscellaneous	1	10	16	38	10	29	27	77
IV. Services	—	8	10	22	2	7	12	37
TOTAL (I+II+III+IV)	61	167	271	489	232	442	564	1,098

Source : Foreign collaboration in Indian Industry, Second Survey Report, 1974, RBI, p. 104

clauses formed 18 per cent. Of the total number of agreements
with regulatory clauses, *viz.*, 654, over 86 per cent or 564 were
those having export restrictive clauses while there was no export
restrictive conditions imposed on the remaining 90 agreements.
Of the 564 agreements with export restrictive clauses, 271 were
for minority companies and 232 for pure technical collaboration
companies while subsidiaries had 61 such agreements.

Country-wise, the proportion of export restrictive agreements
to total agreements was 50 to 60 per cent for the U.K., the
U.S.A., West Germany, France and Italy and was 40 to 50 per
cent for East European countries, Sweden and Netherlands. It
was less than 60 per cent for Japan and Canada (Table 4.4). The
larger number of agreements having export restrictive clauses was
in the manufacturing sector 548 out of 564. Of the former, 310
were in respect of machinery and machine tools (184) and
electrical goods (126). These formed 70 per cent and 60 per cent
respectively of total agreements in these two groups (Table 4.5).
The other industries where export restrictive agreements formed
sizeable proportions were metals and metal products (50 per cent)
and chemicals (30 per cent), the latter mostly on account of basic
industrial chemicals (37 per cent).

Table 4.6
Details Regarding Types of Regulatory Clauses (1964-70)

Type of regulatory clauses	Number of Clauses			
	Subsidiaries	Minority companies	Pure technical companies	Total (1+2+3)
	1	*2*	*3*	*4*
I. Export Clauses of which :—				
(*i*) Permission of collaborator for exports	22	107	73	202
(*ii*) Prohibition of exports to collaborator's country	9	70	77	156

(Contd.)

Table 4.6 (Contd.)

	1	2	3	4
(*iii*) Prohibition of exports to countries in which the collaborator operates through branches/subsidiaries/affiliates or is having similar collaboration agreements	10	112	130	252
(*iv*) Prohibition of exports to countries other than those covered in (*ii*) and (*iii*) above.	5	36	25	66
(*v*) Total ban on exports	—	6	14	20
(*vi*) Exports restricted to certain types of products	—	7	4	11
(*vii*) Exports only through collaborator's agents/distributors	5	14	27	46
(*viii*) Prohibition on the use of trade marks for exports	3	24	26	53
(*ix*) Restriction on the annual value of exports	3	—	—	3
(*x*) Restriction on the annual quantum of exports	—	2	—	2
(*xi*) Restriction on export prices	1	13	—	14
(*xii*) Charging of higher royalty rate for that portion of output which is exported as compared to that on internal sale	—	7	3	10
(*xiii*) Prohibition on the use of technology obtained through the foreign collaboration agreement for export	—	4	2	6
(*xiv*) Any other export restriction	22	55	38	115
Total I	80	457	419	956
II. Conditional payment Clauses				
(*i*) A fixed minimum payment to be made per year	2	11	17	30
(*ii*) payment conditional on achieving a given production target	1	12	9	22

(Contd.)

Table 4.6 (Contd.)

	1	2	3	4
(*iii*) Payments dependent on compulsory exports	2	5	10	17
(*iv*) Other conditions	—	20	5	25
Total II	5	48	41	94
III. Other restrictions				
(*i*) Sources of supply of raw materials and plant and machinery	3	21	28	52
(*ii*) Restriction on production capacity imposed by the collaborator	—	4	15	19
(*iii*) Restriction on manufacture of products similar to those produced under the collaboration agreement	9	56	51	116
(*iv*) Restriction that internal sales should be routed through distributors specified by the collaborator	2	10	6	18
(*v*) Restrictions other than those above	5	22	3	30
Total III	19	113	103	235
Total (I+II+III)	104	618	563	1,285

Source : Foreign Collaboration in Indian Industry Second Survey Report, 1974, RBI, pp. 105-106.

The various types of special clauses can broadly be classified into three groups, namely, exports, conditional payments and others including compulsion in regard to sources of imports, distributors for internal sales, etc. These clauses, in respect of the three groups of private sector companies covered in this study, are set out in Table 4.6. Of the 956 export clauses which restrict exports, nearly two-thirds (610) were those which either (*i*) prohibited exports either to countries where collaborator operated through its branches/subsidiaries/affiliates or had similar collaboration agreements (252), or to collaborator's own country (156) or (*ii*) required collaborator's permission for any exports (202). These restrictions were prominently marked in all the major groups of industries, *viz.*, machinery and machine tools, electrical goods, transport equipment, metals and metal products and chemicals, that is, industries where new technology has to be used as well as in some other industries such as rubber goods. These were almost wholly for minority and pure technical companies. In the case of other agreements, there were 66 clauses whereby exports were restricted not only to countries where the collaborator had subsidiaries or affiliates or to his own country, but also to any other country. However, it can be presumed that in some of these cases, the collaborator kept the right to permit some exports at times. Besides, there were 20 clauses under which exports were totally banned. These were mainly in respect of pure technical collaboration companies (14 out of 20 clauses) and to some extent minority companies (6). Industry-wise, they were distributed among electrical goods, machinery and machine tools and chemical industries. In 53 clauses, use of trademarks for exports was prohibited and these too were in respect of PTCs (26) and minority companies (24), while in 46 clauses, exports were allowed only through the collaborators' agents or distributors, mainly in the case of PTCs (27) and to some extent minority companies (14). The other conditions imposed comprised those which were on export prices (14) and on export or certain types of products (11), and those which charged higher royalty rates on that portion of the output which was exported as compared to that on internal sales (10), or prohibited the use of technology obtained through the foreign collaboration for exports (6) or put a restriction on the annual value and quantum of exports (3 and 2 respectively). Excepting the restriction of annual value of exports which was imposed on subsidiaries (3), all the other restrictions were minority companies and PTCs.

The 94 clauses in regard to conditional payments related mostly to payment of royalty to the collaborator. Thirty of these clauses related to a fixed minimum payment per year, 22 were conditional on achieving a given production target, while 17 related to payments dependent on compulsory exports. Twenty-five clauses were for other conditions. To the extent that these encouraged minimum level of production and exports, these should be welcome. These clauses were in agreements mostly of minority companies (48) and PTCs (41). While the former related more to production targets and other miscellaneous, conditions, for PTCs, they related more to fixed minimum payments and compulsory exports. Among the 'other' (miscellaneous) conditional clauses which numbered 235, the largest number (116) was that on manufacture of products similar to those produced under collaboration agreements and these were mostly for minority companies (56) and PTCs (51.). Clauses restricting sources of supply of raw materials and plant and machinery, *i.e.*, imports, totalled 52 and were mostly for PTCs (28) and minority companies (21). Restrictive clauses on production capacity imposed by the collaborator numbered 19, the largest number (15) being in respect of PTC agreements. The compulsory routing of distribution through collaborators' agents was put in 18 clauses, 10 of which were for minority companies and 6 for PTCs.

A detailed analysis of different clauses in the agreements for major industries showed that for both PTCs and minority companies, export restrictive clauses were predominant in machinery and machine tools (188 and 163 clauses respectively for 87 and 89 agreements). Next in importance was electrical goods and machinery (118 and 90 clauses respectively for minority companies and PTCs) followed by transport equipment (74 and 38 clauses respectively for minority companies and PTCs) (Table 4.7). In the metal and metal products industry, export restrictive clauses were 46 for PTCs and 23 for minority companies while for chemicals and allied products these were 38 for minority companies and 22 for PTCs. These five industries together accounted for over 90 per cent of the total export restrictive clauses for both the minority (457 clauses) and PTC (419 clauses) groups of companies. Electrical goods and machinery and metal and metal products together accounted for 65 per cent of a total of 80 export restrictive clauses for subsidiaries.

A further break-up of export restrictive clauses according to different industries showed that clauses requiring permission of the collaborator for exports and prohibition of exports to collaborator's country or to countries where the collaborator was having branches, subsidiaries or affiliates or had similar collaboration agreements were marked in three industries, namely, machinery and machine tools, electrical goods and transport equipment both in the minority and PTC groups (Table 4.8). The proportion of such restrictive clauses to total export restrictive clauses in each

Table 4.7

Regulatory Clauses in Technical Collaboration Agreements—Industry-wise for Major Categories (1964-70)

Industry / Company group	Items	Transport equip.	Machinery & machine tools	Metals & Metal products	Elect. goods and machinery	Chemicals & Allied Product — Total (including other metals)	Basic industrial	Medicines & pharmaceuticals	Rubber goods	All Industries (including others not shown here)
		1	2	3	4	5	5a	5b	6	7
I. Subsidiaries										
(i)	Export restrictions	9	8	20	32	6	2	2	1	80
(ii)	Conditional payments	—	—	2	1	1	1	1	—	5
(iii)	Others	—	3	6	4	5	1	3	—	19
	Total I	9	11	28	37	12	3	6	1	104
II. Minority Companies										
(i)	Export restrictions	74	163	23	118	38	26	10	1	457
(ii)	Conditional payments	9	3	12	12	3	1	—	—	48
(iii)	Others	12	37	9	27	13	3	6	2	113
	Total II	95	203	44	157	54	30	16	3	618
III. Pure Technical Companies										
(i)	Export restrictions	38	188	46	90	22	8	8	8	419
(ii)	Conditional payments	2	7	10	2	6	4	—	—	41
(iii)	Others	18	31	8	23	15	8	6	4	103
	Total III	58	226	64	115	43	20	14	12	563

Source : Foreign Collaboration in Indian Industry, Second Survey Report, 1974, RBI, p. 109.

Table 4.8

Regulatory Clauses in Technical Collaboration Agreements (By Groups of Companies and Industries) (1964-70)

Industry	Trans-port equip-ment	Machi-nery and machine tools	Metals and metal pro-ducts	Electri-cal goods and machi-nery	Chemicals and allied products			Rubber goods	All indus-tries (inclu-ding those not given sepa-rately here)
					Total (inclu-ding other chemi-cals)	Basic indus-trial	Medi-cines and phar-maceu-ticals		
Clauses	1	2	3	4	5	5a	5b	6	7

A. Minority Companies

I. Export Clauses

	1	2	3	4	5	5a	5b	6	7
(i) Permission of collaborator for exports...	21	37	—	18	22	14	7	—	107
(ii) Prohibition of exports to collaborator's country	9	18	7	25	4	4	—	1	70
(iii) Prohibition of exports to countries in which the collaborator operates through branches/subsidiaries/affiliates or is hav- ing similar collaboration agreements...	18	33	6	30	8	7	—	—	112
(iv) Prohibition of exports to countries other than those covered in (ii) and (iii) above.	8	10	3	12	3	—	—	—	36
(v) Total ban on exports...	—	2	—	—	3	—	3	—	6

Clause									Total
(vi) Exports restricted to certain types of products...	2	1	—	3	—	—	—	—	7
(vii) Exports only through collaborator's agent/distributors...	4	4	—	5	—	—	—	—	14
(viii) Restriction on the use of trademarks...	2	16	—	6	—	—	—	—	24
(ix) Restriction on the annual value of exports...	—	—	—	—	—	—	—	—	—
(x) Restriction on the annual quantum of exports...	1	2	—	—	—	—	—	—	2
(xi) Restriction on export prices...	12	—	—	—	—	—	—	—	13
(xvii) Charging of higher royalty rate for that portion of output which is exported as compared to that on internal sales...	2	1	—	4	—	—	—	—	7
(xiii) Prohibiton on the use of technology obtained through the foreign collaboration agreement for exports...	—	—	—	—	—	—	—	—	7
(xiv) Any other export restriction...	7	27	3	4	15	1	1	—	55
Total I	74	163	23	118	38	26	10	1	457

II. Conditional Payment Clauses

Clause									Total
(i) A fixed minimum payment to be made per year...	1	—	—	2	1	—	—	—	11
(ii) Payment conditional on achieving a given production target...	—	2	—	7	3	—	—	—	12
(iii) Payments dependent on compulsory exports...	—	—	—	3	2	—	—	—	5

(Contd.)

Table 4.8 (Contd)

	1	2	3	4	5	5a	5b	6	7
(vi) Other conditions...	8	1	—	8	1	1	—	—	20
Total II	9	3	12	12	3	1	—	—	48

III. Restrictions other than on Exports

	1	2	3	4	5	5a	5b	6	7
(i) Sources of supply of raw materials and plant and machinery...	3	6	5	4	1	—	1	—	21
(ii) Restrictions on production capacity imposed by the collaborator...	—	—	1	1	1	—	—	—	4
(iii) Restriction on manufacture of products similar to those produced under the collaboration agreement	5	23	3	13	9	3	3	—	56
(iv) Restriction that internal sales should be routed through distributors specified by the collaborators...	—	4	—	1	1	—	1	—	10
(v) Other restrictions...	4	4	—	8	1	—	1	2	22
Total III	12	37	9	27	13	3	6	2	113
Grand Total (I+II+III)	95	203	44	157	54	30	16	3	618

(Contd)

Table 4.8 (Contd.)

Regulatory Clauses in Technical Collaboration Agreements (By Groups of Companies and Industries) (1964-70)

Industry	Transport equipment	Machinery and machine tools	Metals and metal products	Electrical goods and machinery	Chemicals and allied products			Rubber goods	All Industries (including those not given separately here)
					Total (including drug and other chemicals)	Basic industrial chemicals	Medicines and pharmaceuticals		
Clauses	1	2	3	4	5	5a	5b	6	7
B. Pure Technical Companies									
I. Export Clauses									
(i) Permission of Collaborator for exports...	11	36	4	10	4	2	—	—	73
(ii) Prohibition of exports to collaborator's country...	1	42	10	18	2	1	1	1	77
(iii) Prohibition of exports to countries in which the collaborator operates through branches/subsidiaries/affiliates or is having similar collaboration agreements...	17	60	8	31	7	1	5	4	130
(iv) Prohibition of exports to countries other than covered in (ii) and (iii) above...	—	8	14	2	—	—	—	—	25

(Contd.)

Table 4.8 (Contd.)

	1	2	3	4	5	5a	5b	6	7
(v) Total ban on exports... ...	1	—	1	4	3	3	—	3	14
(vi) Exports restricted to certain types of products...	—	—	—	1	—	—	—	—	4
(vii) Exports only through collaborator's agents/distributors...	2	7	—	16	—	—	—	—	27
(viii) Prohibition on the use of trademarks for exports	2	21	—	2	1	—	—	—	26
(ix) Restriction on the annual value of exports...	—	—	—	—	—	—	—	—	—
(x) Restriction on the quantum of exports.	—	—	—	—	—	—	—	—	—
(xi) Restriction on export prices... ...	—	—	—	—	—	—	—	—	—
(xii) Charging of higher royalty rate for that portion of output which is exported as compared to that on internal sales ...	1	—	—	—	2	—	2	—	3
(xiii) Prohibition on the use of technology obtained through the foreign collaboration agreement for exports...	—	—	1	1	—	—	—	—	2
(xiv) Any other export restriction...	3	14	8	5	3	1	—	—	38
Total I	38	188	46	90	22	8	8	8	419

(*Contd.*)

II. Conditional Payment Clauses

									Total
(i) A fixed minimum payment to be made per year...	1	3	4	—	1	—	—	—	17
(ii) Payment conditional on achieving a given production target...	—	—	2	2	1	1	—	—	9
(iii) Payments dependent on compulsory exports...	1	3	1	—	3	3	—	—	10
(iv) Other conditions...	—	1	3	—	1	—	—	—	5
Total II ...	2	7	10	2	6	4	—	—	41

III. Restrictions other than on Exports

									Total
(i) Sources of supply of raw materials and plant and machinery...	1	3	1	18	—	—	3	2	28
(ii) Restriction on production capacity imposed by the collaborator...	1	—	3	—	11	8	3	—	15
(iii) Restriction on manufacture of products similar to those produced under the collaboration agreement...	16	21	4	4	4	—	3	2	51
(iv) Restriction that internal sales should be routed through distributors specified by collaborator...	—	—	6	—	—	—	—	—	6
(v) Restrictions other than those above ...	—	1	—	1	1	—	—	—	3
Total III ...	18	31	8	23	15	8	6	4	103
Grand Total (I+II+III)...	58	226	64	115	43	20	14	12	563

(Contd.)

Table 4.8 (Contd.)

Regulatory Clauses in Technical Collaboration Agreements (By Groups of Companies and Industries (1964-70)

	1	2	3	4	5	5a	5b	6	7
C. Subsidiaries									
I. Export Clauses									
(i) Permission of collaborator for exports...	1	5	6	3	3	1	2	1	22
(ii) Prohibition of exports to collaborator's country...	1	—	3	4	—	—	—	—	9
(iii) Prohibition of exports to countries in which the collaborator operates through branches/subsidiaries/affiliates or is having similar collaboration agreements...	1	2	5	2	—	—	—	—	10
(iv) Prohibition of exports to countries other than covered in (ii) and (iii) above... ...	—	—	5	—	—	—	—	—	5
(v) Total ban on exports...	—	—	—	—	—	—	—	—	—
(vi) Exports restricted to certain types of products...	—	—	—	—	—	—	—	—	—
(vii) Exports only through collaborator's agents/distributors...	1	—	—	3	1	—	—	—	5
(viii) Prohibition on the use of trademark for exports...	1	—	—	2	—	—	—	—	3

									Total
(ix) Restriction on the annual value of exports...	—	—	—	—	3	—	—	—	3
(x) Restriction on the annual quantum of exports...	—	—	—	—	—	2	—	—	2
(xi) Restriction on export prices... ...	1	—	—	1	—	—	—	—	1
(xii) Charging of higher royalty rate for that portion of output which is exported as compared to that on internal sales... ...	—	—	20	—	—	—	—	—	—
(xiii) Prohibition on the use of technology obtained through the foreign collaboration agreement for exports...	—	1	15	—	2	1	1	2	22
(xiv) Any other export restriction...	3	1	1	—	2	1	1	—	22
Total I...	9	8	20	1	32	6	2	2	80

II. Conditional Payment Clauses

									Total
(i) A fixed minimum payment to be paid per year...	—	1	—	—	—	—	—	—	2
(ii) Payment conditional on achieving a given production target... ...	—	—	1	—	—	—	—	—	1
(iii) Payments dependent on compulsory exports...	—	1	—	1	1	—	1	—	2
(iv) Other conditions...	—	—	—	—	—	—	—	—	—
Total II	—	2	1	1	1	—	1	—	5

(Contd.)

Table 4.8 Contd.

	1	2	3	4	5	5a	5b	6	7
III. Restrictions other than on Exports									
(i) Sources of supply of raw materials and plant and machinery...	—	—	2	—	1	—	—	—	3
(ii) Restriction on production capacity imposed by the collaborator...	—	—	—	—	—	—	—	—	—
(iii) Restriction on manufacture of products similar to those produced under the collaboration agreement...	—	1	2	4	2	—	2	—	9
(iv) Restriction that internal sales should be routed through distributors specified by the collaborator...	—	2	—	—	—	—	—	—	2
(v) Restrictions other than those above...	—	—	2	—	2	1	1	—	5
Total III...	3	3	6	4	5	1	3	—	19
Grand Total (I+II+III)	9	11	28	37	12	3	6	1	104

Source : Foreign Collaboration in Indian Industry, Second Survey Report, RBI, 1974, pp. 110-115.

of these three industries ranged between 54 per cent and 65 per cent for the minority group and 66 per cent and 76 per cent for the PTCs. Clauses whereby exports were restricted to countries other than those where the collaborator had branches, subsidiaries or affiliates or to his own country were prominent in the case of electrical goods, machinery and machine tools and transport equipment industries for the minority group and metals and metal products and machinery and machine tools industries for the PTCs ; such clauses for subsidiary companies were only in one industry, namely metals and metal products. The use of trademarks for exports was prohibited mainly in machinery and machine tools both for the minority companies and PTC groups. Clauses banning exports totally were 14 in PTCs, 6 in minority companies and none in subsidiaries as compared with 18 in PTCs, 15 in minority companies and 3 in subsidiaries in 1963-64. The decline in the number of such clauses in 1969-70 reflected perhaps the shift in the Government policy in regard to approvals for foreign collaboration so as to ensure that clauses banning exports did not feature in agreements of recent years. Industry-wise, clauses banning exports in the PTC group were largely in respect of electrical goods, basic industrial chemicals and rubber goods industries. A further break-down showed that these clauses were in such lines of manufactures as miniature circuit breakers, conductors, flexible shafts, gear and auxiliary equipments in the electrical goods industry, urea and phenol formaldehyde resin and formaldehyde explosives in the basic chemical industry, life saving equipment, oil seals of synthetic and natural rubber and rubber closures for injection bottles in the rubber goods industry. In the case of the minority group, such clauses were noticed in companies manufacturing cosmetics and cosmetic specialities and certain kinds of vitamins as also automatic looms and plant and machinery parts for the cement industry.

Restrictions on sources of imports of raw materials and machinery were predominant in PTCs with 28 clauses followed by minority companies with 21 clauses. Subsidiaries had only 3 such clauses. It is interesting to note that 18 of the 28 clauses of the PTCs were concentrated in the electrical goods and machinery industry in such individual lines of manufacture as electrical wires and cables, dry cell batteries, low voltage circuits, diffusers for sugarcane, milk coolers, can washers, bottle washing and filling machines, condensed milk plants, centrifugal milk pumps, solvent extraction plants, feed milling plant, film cooling tower, spray drying plants, etc. The 21 clauses of the minority group were largely distributed among machinery and machine tools, metals and metal products and electrical goods and machinery. The individual items of manufacture were pistons, autoshock-absorbers, motor cycles, boilers and pressure vessels, water tube boilers, cement plant and parts under machinery and machine tools, aluminium ingots, bars, wire and wire ropes, under metals and metal products and radio components, TV receivers, tape recorders and components, X-ray equipment and alloy magnets, fluoroscopic and intensifying screens under electrical goods and machinery.

Restriction on manufacture of products similar to those produced under the collaboration agreements were predominant both in the minority and PTC groups with 56 and 51 clauses respectively. There were only 9 such clauses for the subsidiary group. Industry-wise, these clauses were largely in machinery and machine tools, electrical goods and machinery and chemicals in the minority group and in machinery and machine tools and transport equipment in the PTC group. A further breakdown showed that the individual items of manufacture under machinery and machine tools were filtration equipment, tobacco processing equipment, air compressors, water ring vaccum pumps and blowers, industrial furnaces, water tube boilers, cellulose board and paper plants, cotton spinning and worsted spinning machinery, diesel engines, etc. Fans and blowers, air handling units, welding electrodes, X-ray equipment and alloys magnets, textometors and motor starters were some of the items under electrical goods and machinery while items under chemicals were dyes and intermediates, specialised chemical for pretreatment of metals, vitreous enamel ceramic colours, salicylic acid and salicylates as well as pharmaceuticals and agrochemicals. In the pure technical group such restrictions were largely in autolooms and components, winding and weaving machines, oil engines, slotting machines, boilers, industrial fans, field furnaces, automatic cutting lathes, threading machines, industrial fans, grinding machines, etc. under machinery and machine tools, and in auto accessories and spare parts, gear motors, gear boxes, clutches, taximeters, passenger cars, diesel engines, etc. under transport equipment.

Restriction that internal sales should be routed through distributors specified by the collaborator was mainly in respect of machinery and machine tools for both the minority and PTC groups and it was noticed in such individual items of manufacture as grinding machines, autolooms and components, winding and weaving machines, winding and wharping creel, power presses, filtration equipment, hard tools and allied products and tractor and tractor parts.

It would be interesting to assess the restrictive clauses relating to agreements covered in this Survey in comparison with those covered in the preceding Survey. The data on restrictive clauses in the two survey periods are, however, not strictly comparable because of the difference in the type of coverage of such clauses in the questionnaire of the two Surveys. Nevertheless, an attempt is made here to broadly compare the major restrictive clauses. Total number of restrictive clauses for the three groups of private sector companies during 1964-70 was higher at 1,285 as compared to 750 during 1960-64 ; of these, the share of subsidiaries, minority companies and PTCs was 104, 618 and 563 respectively, during 1964-70 as against 80, 334 and 336 during 1960-64. Bulk of the restrictive clauses in all the three groups of companies related to export restrictions. In the case of subsidiaries export restrictive clauses were 80 during 1964-70 accounting for 77 per cent of the total number of restrictive clauses of this group as against 56 clauses or 70 per cent during 1960-64 ; such clauses for minority companies and PTCs were 457 (74 per cent) and 419 (74 per cent) respectively, during 1964-70 as against 230 (69 per cent) and 169 (50 per cent) during 1960-64 (Table 4.9). The increase in the export restrictive clauses has been mainly accounted for by a large number of clauses prohibiting exports to collaborator's country or to countries in which the collaborator operated through branches/subsidiaries/affiliates or was having similar collaboration agreements.* These clauses requiring permission of the collabora-

---

* Part of the increase in these clauses over the two survey periods may be statistical as it was due to the assumption of same number of clauses in agreements of those companies which had more than one agreement but which failed to furnish agreement-wise details.

Table 4.9
Types of Regulatory Clauses (by Groups of Companies for 1960-64 and 1964-70)

Type of restriction	Subsidiary companies — Number of clauses/agreements				Minority companies — Number of clauses/agreements				Pure technical companies — Number of clauses/agreements			
	1960-64		1964-70		1960-64		1964-70		1960-64		1964-70	
	No. of clauses/agreements	percentage to total	No. of clauses/agreements	percentage to total	No. of clauses/agreements	percentage to total	No. of clauses/agreements	percentage to total	No. of clauses/agreements	percentage to total	No. of clauses/agreements	percentage to total
A. Total number of agreements	144		167		445		489		462		442	
B. Total number of agreements with regulatory of A ...	63		68		251		320		213		266	
C. B as percentage of A	43.8		40.7		56.4		65.4		46.1		60.2	
Total clauses	80	100.0	104	100.0	334	100.0	618	100.0	336	100.0	563	100.0
I. Export clauses	56	70.0	80	76.9	230	68.9	457	73.9	169	50.3	419	74.4
(1) Permission of collaborator for exports	32	40.0	22	21.1	80	24.0	107	17.3	37	11.0	73	13.0
(2) Exports prohibited only to certain countries	3	3.8	24*	23.1	17	5.1	218*	35.3	22	6.6	232*	41.2
(3) Export prohibited	3	3.8	—	—	15	4.5	6	0.9	18	5.3	14	2.5
(4) Exports restricted to certain types of products	1	1.2	—	—	2	0.6	7	1.1	1	0.3	4	0.7
(5) Exports restricted only to collaborator's agents/distributors	1	1.2	5	4.8	13	3.9	14	2.3	6	1.8	27	4.8
(6) Others including those only to certain countries	16	20.0	29	27.9	103	30.8	105	17.0	85	25.3	69	12.2
II. Sources of supply of raw materials plant of machinery	14	17.5	3	2.9	46	13.7	21	3.4	94	28.0	28	5.0
III. Restrictions on production pattern	2	2.5	—	—	36	10.8	4	0.7	27	8.0	15	2.7
IV. Payment of minimum royalty	1	1.2	2	1.9	14	4.2	11	1.8	40	11.9	17	3.7
V. Other restrictions	7	8.8	19	18.3	8	2.4	125	20.2	6	1.8	84	14.9

*The large number of clauses may partly be due to the assumption of same number of clauses in agreements of those companies which had more than one agreement but which failed to furnish agreement-wise details.

Source : Foreign Collaboration in Indian Industry, Second Survey Report, RBI, 1974, pp. 118,

tors for exports showed a decline from 32 for the last Survey to 22 for this Survey for subsidiaries while they had shown an increase both in the case of minority (from 80 to 107) and PTC (from 37 to 73) groups. There was a decline in the number of clauses which banned exports altogether during the two survey

Table 4.10
Developing Countries with Different Types of Export Restrictions

Types of Export Restrictions	Countries
Export Restrictions (General)[1]	: Brazil, Chile, Columbia, El Salvedor, Ghana, Guatamala, Honduras, India, Kuwait, Malta, Mexico, Pakistan, Philippines, Singapore
Global ban on exports	: Brazil, Columbia, Guatemala, Kuwait, India, Mexico, Pakistan.
Exports prohibited to specified countries	: India, Mexico, Pakistan, : Singapore
Exports permitted to specified countries	: Brazil, El Salvedor, Guatemala, Honduras, India, Iran, Kuwait, Malta, Mexico
Prior approval for exports	: India, Mexico, Pakistan, Philippines
Export quotas	: Columbia, India, Mexico
Exports restricted to specified products	: Columbia, India
Exports permitted through or to specified firms only	: Honduras, India
Price controls on exports	: Columbia, India, Mexico, Pakistan
Exports of substitute products probihited	: Columbia, Philippines
Tied purchases	: Brazil, Columbia, India, Philippines
Restrictions on production pattern	: Columbia, India, Mexico, Philippines
Restrictions on disclosures	: Brazil, India

Source : UNCTAD, Restrictive Business Practices, 1971, p. 19.

1. A few countries noted the existence of export restrictions in general terms with no specification as to type. These countries plus those that specified types of restrictions, are included in this category.

periods ; such clauses were 6 in minority companies, 14 in PTCs and none in subsidiaries during 1964-70 as against 15, 18 and 3 respectively, during 1960-64. It is also interesting to note that over the two periods there was a decline in the number of clauses stipulating sources of supply of raw materials and plant and machinery as well ; such clauses declined from 94 to 28 for PTCs, 46 to 21 for minority companies and 14 to 3 for subsidiaries during the two survey period.

The various types of restrictions in the collaboration agreements discussed in the foregoing paragraphs are pervasive in nature and cover not only the production and distributive activity of the companies but also their export activity. The restrictions on exports in the collaboration agreements implied that the foreign collaborators desired to manufacture largely for domestic consumption. Also, restrictions such as those on production capacity, manufacture of products similar to those produced under the collaboration agreement and the absence of freedom in the choice of distributors both for internal as well as external sales were not conducive to expansion of production and sales of these industrial units. However, these drawbacks have to be weighed against any benefit derived in the form of import substitution in the domestic market and supply of new technology. Considering that the various export restrictive clauses are relevant for a limited period after which the Indian Company could dispense with all the most sophisticated technology imparted by the foreign collaborator by training its own personnel and developing its own research, disadvantages of seeking foreign collaboration seem to be of a kind which are likely to be minimised over a period of time.

Restrictive clauses in other developing countries are as common as they are in India. A view can be had from the Table 4.10.

DEVELOPMENT IMPLICATIONS OF THE RBPs

For discussing the various implications of the restrictive business practices in overall development following manifestations of development can be considered :

Rural Development : The most central feature of under-development is to be found in the rural political economy of the developing countries. The relevance of the RBPs of multinational corporations to rural development emanates from the fact that the corporations have been able to monopolise large holdings of land (often the more productive ones) and that this, it could be reasoned, has deprived other socio-economic groups from having access to comparable resources. They have also been able to hold monopolistic conditions in the labour markets in the developing countries, thus enabling them to influence the determination of rural wage rates and conditions of work to an important extent. Evidences can be seen in the Caribbean countries to support this.

However, in India this aspect has a limited scope except in few of the States where commercial crops have been subject to monopolistic control of the MNCs (like tea, rubber plantations). But the conclusion that emerge from this phenomena is wherever MNCs have worked in plantation sector they have definitely distorted the rural labour market and exacerbated the inequalities rural income distribution.

Natural Resource Development : Implications of RBPs with regard to natural resource development is based on the fact that foreign ownership of strategic and/or non-renewable resources may operate against long-term national development objective of the developing countries. Chile, where studies were made for copper and bauxite has confirmed this view where some evidences have suggested that very limited processing took place, high profits were repatriated and the overall contribution to development was extremely limited.[19] Same was the case with tin in Malaysia. Pre-nationalisation situations of crude oil production in India has the same story to tell. This industry has a unique example of repatriating profits many times of original investment whereas the contribution to national development was minimal.

It is true that such MNC's bring in the latest technology and systems of operations in exploration and refining that tend to enjoy competitive advantage over local firms. It could be argued

---

19. See the studies by Girvan, N., 'Copper in Chile', Mona, University of West Indies, 1972.

that control over such key resources by a few firms has enabled such firms to dictate the rule of game not only in terms of competition but also over rewards and concessions from the government. If this is so, RBPs would seem to have a crucial role to play not only in the process of the monopolisation of these firms but also in the power this process confers on the respective firms. It is true that productivity would tend to be higher than in competitive local firms using old technology, for example, however, this does not come in the way of the validity of the point.

Output : It is a fact that oligopolies and/or collusive monopolies can maximise profits only by restricting total output. This, ultimately, is likely to reduce economic growth and, therefore, to affect the common well-being of the developing nations. Both growth and well being are critical issues in developing countries. Growth in real output is necessary to relieve absolute poverty levels in such countries. It is a fact that the limitation on output has been a common form of RBP used by the multinational corporations in the less developed countries.

Employment : A common feature of RBPs may be the reduction of output. Keeping in view the labour intake of the firms is likely to be less than in more competitive conditions. If this is so, then the employment boundary within given production techniques is not extended to the fullest possible extent. Moreover, employment of capital-intensive techniques, as it does, of production also limits the possibility of absorption of surplus labour in developing countries. Further, we see that RBP also limits the employment creation of certain key skills locally. It may be the part of their strategy, for example, access to the knowledge and confirming the local people upto a certain level of management. It happens commonly in high technology industries such as chemicals, engineering and electronics. Thus the process of human capital formation is restricted to a great extent in the developing countries. The International Labour Organisation (ILO) in a resolution called on the MNCs to adopt more positive attitude towards offering employment opportunities to the nationals of the developing countries in key areas.[20]

---

20. ILO, 'Tripartite Declarations of Principles Covering Multinational Enterprises and Social Policy', Geneva, 1977.

Income Distribution : Adoption of the RBPs and mono-polising the market thereby helps the MNCs to obtain disproportionately large amount of income derived from profits. Due to the RBPs the foreign firms are able to charge higher than normal prices for products or services and as a result able to earn supernormal profits. Income distribution can be affected at the following levels—between foreign-market dominated enterprises *vis-a-vis* smaller local producers in the same market and between foreign firms *vis-a-vis* wage earners and other groups. MNCs pay higher wages than the local firms do in similar industries and thus an element of inequality of income is introduced. This not only results in disorganising the labour market but also destroys the local firms even if the higher wages have been paid by the MNCs as a predatory attempt to obtain sufficient local labour. There are certain studies which have confirmed the monopoly earning capacities of market dominating transnational firms in the developing countries.[21]

Resource Allocation: Studies on industrial organisation and corporate performance show that RBPs result in lower economic efficiency than would occur in competitive conditions. Several international resolutions have, therefore, urged MNCs to adopt a more "host country-oriented resource-sourcing pattern." The adoption of foreign input sourcing of MNCs appears to be the most frequent in vertically integrated enterprises especially those engaged in assembly-type operations—hence, high degree of intra-firm trade is often found there. On the other hand full utilisation of local resources is vital to enhance economic development possibilities in developing countries because this process can render the structure of production more heterogenous by spreading economic activities cross sectionally through various forms of linkages. It becomes all the more important with the developing countries having the characteristic of being primary producers and lacking diversity in domestic production structure.

There are so many other implications in terms of which the role and impact of RBPs could be considered such as, welfare effects of price ; effects on local competitions ; import substitu-

---

21. Vaitsos, C.V., "Inter-country Income Distribution and Transnational Enterprises', Oxford, Oxford University Press, 1974.

tion ; export promotion, etc. etc. All the dimensions discussed above are by no means comprehensive but surely helps in understanding the magnitude of the problem. Also the consequences, no doubt, will vary from country to country depending on nature and their relationship with the multinational corporations.

CONCLUSION

The whole world can be divided into two so far as the restrictive business practices are concerned. One, the RBP intensive sector, represented by developing countries and second, non-RBP sector represented by developed countries. However, the latter countries too have RBPs but incidence of such practices are higher in case of the former. It goes without saying that the RBPs used by the multinational corporations are a great threat to the host countries' economies and they must be checked before they go against the economic development requirement of the country. Various types of RBPs used by the MNCs, in one way or the other, should be effectively checked either through legislative action or administrative acumen. Many RBPs have diverted the meagre economic resources of the countries to non-developmental channels. Moreover, the multinational corporations are reaping advantages from the use of natural resources of the host countries which could have been otherwise used for these countries.

MULTINATIONAL CORPORATIONS AND BALANCE OF PAYMENTS

5

Multinational Corporations and Balance of Payments

INTRODUCTION

At the very beginning of the discussion one primary question knocks our attention : whether the balance of payment effects should be considered separately from real income effects ? The distinction between these two effects may be blurred in the long run, yet it would be correct to identify these two effects separately in short run perspective. In fact, the developing countries do not find it convenient to use various adjustment mechanisms needed for the survival in a world of 'second best' solutions. Even if the domestic resources are found adequate to meet the investment targets, the economies are too rigid to allow the price income adjustments to close down the foreign exchange gap.[1] Therefore, if the multinational corporations add significantly to the output of the developing countries (or host countries), it does not necessarily mean that the impact on balance of payment will also be positive.

Among the many dimensions of the impact of the multinational corporations one most important dimension is their implications on host countries' balance of payments. The inflow and outflow of total foreign exchange resources are generally recorded on the balance of payment sheet of a country. Though the total inflow and outflow of foreign exchange are not taken

---

1. Chenery, H. and Strout, A., 'Foreign Assistance and Economic Development', American Economic Review, LVI, September 1966, pp. 680-733.

into account here, only that part of the flow is taken into account which is contributed or perpetuated by the multinational corporations.

Balance of payment is affected by MNCs' operations through various investments, transfer of technology, transfer pricing, foreign remittances in the form of royalties, fees, commission, dividends and travelling expenses in foreign currency. On the basis of various studies conducted by some forums and economists it has been confirmed that the net impact of these multinational corporations' operations have been negative on the balance of payment (BOP) of the host countries.

While considering the balance of payment effects not only investment flows but trade flows are also to be considered so as to give the better picture about the balance of payment effects. One study of 159 samples[2] has revealed that 145 (91 per cent)

Table 5.1
Balance of Payment Impact on Six Development Countries

Country	Samples	Negative impact on balance of payment
Jamaica	11	8
Kenya	8	3
India	53	48
Malaysia	15	14
Iran	16	16
Columbia	56	56
Total	159	145

Source : Extracted and consolidated from the study of Lall, Sanjay and Streeton, Paul.

2. Bergsten, C. Fred., 'An Analysis of US Foreign Direct Investment Policy and Economic Development', Brooking Institution, Nov. 1975. But seems to have been quoted originally from the study of Paul Streeton and Sanjay Lall, 'Summary of Methods and Findings of Study of Private Foreign Manufacturing Investments in 6 developing Countries, Geneva, UNCTAD, May 1973 (in 3 parts), Part 1, Methodology used in Studies on Private Foreign Investment in Selected Developing Countries, TD/B/C 3(vi)/Misc. 6, p. 1.

cases revealed negative balance of payment impact on the economy of the host countries. It may be seen from the Table 5.1. Vaitsos has brilliantly elucidated how the transfer pricing practices used by the MNCs have caused the drain on foreign exchange resources of the host countries especially the developing ones[3] and making their balance of payment position precarious.

Restrictive trade practices are another factor contributing to the adverse impact on balance of payments.[4] The main impact on balance of payment consists of the export and re-import of capital by parent companies and within company groups and the transfer of income on this capital. 'Capital' comprises all financial resources, whether in the form of equity or loan capital supplied to subsidiaries, branches and associated companies abroad. 'Income' comprises return on capital, *i.e.*, all remittances of dividends, loan interest and profit from branches.

EFFECTS ON CAPITAL ACCOUNT AND INVESTMENT INCOME ACCOUNT

The impact of the operation of the MNCs on the balance of payment of host countries may be discussed from two angles ; one is their impact on capital account and investment income account, and the other is their effect on the generation of exports and imports, *i.e.*, on the trade flows. The balance of payment of the host countries gets a significant relief when the MNCs make an investment. But on the other hand, it deteriorates when dividends, royalties and technical fees are repatriated or amortisations are made. Had inward flow of investment been larger than the outflows every time the question of weakening of the balance of payment would not have arisen. But the evidences are mostly to the contrary. In fact, the problem lies both with the outflows and inflows. The inward flow of investment that is expected to improve the balance of payment position does not represent wholly the inflow in cash. A good part of it is the inflow in kind and in that case, if the transfer is shown at inflated

---

3. Vaitsos, C.V., 'Inter country Income Distribution and Transnational Corporations', Oxford, Clarendon Press, 1974.
4. Long, Frank, 'Restrictive Business Practices, TNCs and Development— A Survey', Martinus Nijhoff Publishing, Boston,1981.

price, the figures of investment swell to that extent without any real gain to the balance of payment.

Table 5.2 shows the regional inflow and outflow of resources in the form of profits, dividends, royalties and technical fees, etc. and the net impact thereof.

Table 5.2
Region-wise Inflow and Outflow of Resources (1970-1979)

(Million of US $)

	Inflow	Outflow	Balance
Africa	270.7	996.2	—725.5
W. Hemisphere	228.0	936.0	—708.0
Asia and West Asia	200.1	2,401.9	—2,201.8

Source : The UN Document No. 7, pp. 192-193.

In India also the Reserve Bank of India has confirmed that negative impact on balance of payment[5] due to foreign companies was for Rs. 8,910 million during 1964-70 where foreign companies have remitted more than 232 per cent that of inflow. The Indian situation will be discussed in detail later in this chapter.

At the same time, the amount of profit generated is determined by the amount of total investment in the affiliates. The inflow of funds from the parent organisations forms only a part of such total investment. The other important segment is local, of which ploughing back of profit figures large. In the initial years, the ploughing back of profit minimises the burden of profit repatriation, but in the long run, it aggravates the problem. It is because as the profits are ploughed back every year, the amount of total investments expands and thereby the generation of the profit amount increases. As a consequence, larger amount of profit are repatriated involving larger amount of foreign exchange. Table 5.3 provides an illustration on the assumption that total income earned is 15 per cent. Half of such income is re-invested and the other half is repatriated. At the same time amortisation takes place every year at the rate of 5 per cent. Again fresh capital inflows are constant—being 100 crores of

5. RBI Bulletin, June 1974.

Table 5.3
Impact of a Constant Inflow of Foreign Capital on the Balance of Payment

(Rupees in crores)

Year	Fresh capital inflow	Total capital in the beginning of the year: (7) of previous year plus (2) of current yr.	Amortisation of capital at the rate of 5 per cent	Profits at the rate of 15 per cent	Re-investment of profits	Total book value of foreign investment at the end of the year (3)+(6)—(4)	Transfer abroad of investment income	Total outpayments for service charges and repatriation (4)+(8)	Net results on the capital account of the balance of payments (2)—(9)
1	*2*	*3*	*4*	*5*	*6*	*7*	*8*	*9*	*10*
1.	100	100.00	5.00	15.00	7.50	102.50	7.50	12.50	87.50
2.	100	202.50	10.13	30.38	15.19	207.56	15.19	25.32	74.68
3.	100	307.56	15.38	46.13	23.07	315.25	23.07	38.45	61.55
4.	100	415.25	20.77	62.29	31.15	425.63	31.15	51.92	48.08
5.	100	525.63	26.28	78.84	39.42	538.77	39.42	65.70	34.30
6.	100	638.77	31.94	95.81	47.90	686.67	47.90	79.84	20.16
7.	100	786.67	39.33	117.99	59.00	806.34	59.00	98.33	1.67
8.	100	906.34	45.31	135.94	67.97	929.00	67.97	113.28	—13.28
9.	100	1,029.00	51.45	154.35	77.18	1,054.73	77.18	128.63	—28.63
10.	100	1,154.73	57.74	173.22	86.61	1,183.60	86.61	144.35	—44.35
11.	100	1,283.60	64.18	192.54	96.27	1,315.69	96.27	160.45	—60.45
12.	100	1,415.69	70.78	212.34	106.17	1,451.08	106.17	176.95	—76.95
13.	100	1,551.08	77.55	232.65	116.32	1,589.85	116.32	193.87	—93.80
14.	100	1,689.85	84.49	253.47	126.73	1,732.09	126.73	211.22	—111.22

rupees a year. This shows that only in eighth year, the out-payments exceed fresh capital inflows. In the 14th year the former doubles the magnitude of the latter.

CHARGES FOR TRANSFER OF TECHNOLOGY

The other factor straining the balance of payment of the host country is the charges paid for the technology by the affiliates or subsidiaries or branches of foreign companies. Technology is transferred in two ways : one in the form of such industrial property rights as patents, process techniques, designs and the like ; the other in the form of technical training concerned with it. The licensing agreements stipulate that the licensee pays a royalty for the patents, know-how or trade marks and also technical fees. The agreement provides also for the mode of payment. If royalty is paid in lump sum, the external reserves are affected only once. If it is paid as percentage of the licensee's net sales of the licensed product over the life of contract (as it generally happens in most of the technical collaboration agreements) the payment exerts a continuous pressure on external reserve position of the country in question, but only for the period of contract which is generally of 5 to 10 years yet in some cases, the agreement additionally provides for the sale of licensed product to the parent company at a lower than that of arm's length price. This serves to be an additional burden on foreign exchange reserves yet again, the charges are sometimes convertible into equity shares of the affiliate. This causes permanent drainage from the foreign exchange reserves and such payments naturally increase with the rise in profit and sales. According to an UNCTAD study the direct payments for the technology made by the developing countries come around 1.5 billion US dollars per aunum, which is more than that of annual increase in their export earnings.

The study on transfer of technology (Chapter 3) has already confirmed that the foreign companies have lower export performance index as compared to the domestic firms. At the same time the former have greater import intensity than the latter. It shows that the capacity of foreign companies to contribute to 'credits' side of the balance of payment is limited and on the other hand they contribute heavily on the 'debit' side because of having high import intensity. This has undisputably established that overall contribution of foreign companies to the balance of payment has been negative.

THE TRADE FLOWS

Apart from the effects on the capital and investment income accounts, balance of payment of the host country is influenced by the quantum and pattern of trade of these multinational corporations. It is determined by the policy of MNCs, the policy of host governments and the organisational relationship between parent company and the affiliate. If the objective of the MNCs behind the very investment is to meet the local demand, the possibility of export augmentation would be meagre and particularly when they impose various restrictions on exports for this purpose. On the other hand the import bill will be large if the very objective is to find a market for the goods produced by the parent company. Again, if the host government invites the MNCs for import substitution, any export is possible after the domestic demand is satiated. The export is dependent also upon how far the host government provides export incentives. As far as the organisational relationship is concerned, it may be horizontal or vertical. On horizontal lines, the MNCs are found investing in the manufacture of final products. The final products may possibly be exported after satisfying the domestic demand as they get an additional advantage of internationally known brands and trade marks. But since the export of final products from developing countries meet high tariff walls, quotas and retaliations in the developed market despite the UNCTAD sponsored GSP, the MNCs prefer to take up the manufacturing operations in the developing host countries under this broad vertically integrated set up.[6]

The MNCs are generally powerful enough to co-ordinate the activities of their affiliates spreading over a number of countries for their common good. In order to minimise the cost of their

---

6. Helleiner, G.K., 'Manufactured Exports from Less Developed Countries and Multinational firms', Economic Journal, LXXXIII, March 1973, pp. 21-47. ; Leontiades, James, 'International Sourcing in the LDCs', Columbia Journal of World Business, VI, Sept.-Oct., 1971, pp. 19-28 ; Stikker, D.U., 'The Role of Private Enterprises in Investment and Promotion of Exports in Developing Countries', New York, UN, 1968.

overall operations, they locate in different countries different stages of production processes and thereby determine the flow of trade. We can make it clear with the help of a hypothetical example. As MNC is incorporated in country 'A' which subsequently sets up its affiliate in country 'B' which is a low wage economy. The country 'A' is a high wage economy on the one hand and has a higher tariff on finished goods on the other but a much lower tariff on imports of components. In this case raw material will flow from the MNC in country 'A' to 'B' and in collaboration with other local materials, the components will be manufactured in country 'B'. They will be exported to country 'A' for their assembly into a finished product. The finished products will be sold with high profits behind the protective tariff wall. It may even be profitable to export back the assembled units to country 'B' if there are comparatively low tariffs levied on finished goods. Again if the tariff provisions in country 'A' provide for a low tariff on the import of those finished goods whose components are manufactured in country 'A', in that case too, it would be cheaper for an MNC in country 'A' to set up its affiliate in country 'B' to export components to its affiliate and import back the assembled units.[7] This has given rise to intra-firm trade at a growing rate. Mechanism and implications of such trade have already been discussed in Chapter 4.

But a very important factor comes in picture that makes the intra-firm trade beneficial to parent companies generally at the cost of the balance of payment of the host countries. Since the various affiliates of the MNCs are closely integrated, they can easily manipulate the trade for the maximisation of the global profit. They do it by means of under-invoicing and over-invoicing generally known as transfer pricing mechanism. If the affiliate has to transfer funds to the parent organisation through the price channel, the goods coming from the parent company is overpriced or the goods going from the affiliate is under-priced. By this device the exports do not add to the foreign exchange reserves to the extent they are underpriced and imports artificially made dearer because of overpricing prove to be a drain on foreign exchange reserves.

---

7.   Such instances are found in the US under tariff items 806.30 and 807.90.

INDIAN CASE

The growing influence of the multinational corporations in the Indian economy can in no case be ignored. It is not only that India plays host to a good number of multinational corporations, their stock have grown faster than the country's gross domestic product (GDP). But when we attempt to identify their economic effects, especially on the balance of payments, non-availability of data poses a serious predicament. The foreign firms always fought shy in disclosing the information as it goes against their business ethos. Thus the secondary sources of RBI publications and others were considered as the data base for the purpose.

The MNCs operate in India either through their branches or through investing in, and controlling, the companies incorporated in India (called as subsidiaries of foreign controlled rupee companies or FCRCs). The study has been divided into two parts— one for the ten years' period ending March 1974 and another for the period 1975-76 to 1977-78.

Period ending March 1974

During this period the outstanding investment in branches remained almost constant with yearly fluctuation between Rs. 280 crores and Rs. 218.8 crores. On the contrary those in FCRCs rose by more than 200 per cent from Rs. 305.8 crores to Rs. 671.8 crores during the same period. In the manufacturing sector, which attracted the larget share of foreign investment during this period, FCRCs shared about 90 per cent of the investment.[8]

INFLOWS AND OUTFLOWS

Let us take first the case of branches. During the six year period between 1964-65 and 1969-70 there was net dis-investment of Rs. 39.4 crores baring the year of 1964-65 in which there was net inflow of Rs. 2.1 crore which is quite an insignificant. The total outflow of funds was still larger (Rs. 97 crores) because profits were repatriated to the tune of Rs. 59.7 crores during the same period (Table 5.4).

In case of FCRCs, the total inflow of investment in equity during 1964-70 amounted to Rs. 80 crores, about one-sixth of

---

8. RBI Bulletin, July 1975 and March 1978.

Table 5.4

Inflows and Outflows on Capital and Investment Income Accounts of Branches and Foreign Subsidiaries in India

(Amount in crores of Rupees)

	BRANCHES			Investment in Equity*			Net Invest- ment in Equity	SUBSIDIARIES OUTFLOWS					Col. 13 as % of Col. 8
Year	Net Invest- ment	Profits repatri- ated	Net out- flow of funds	Cash	Kind	Total		Divi- dend	Royal- ties	Tech. Fees	Pay ments to Fr. Techni- cians	Total	
1	2	3	4	5	6	7	8	9	10	11	12	13	14
1964-65	2.1	13.8	11.7	2.2	20.2	22.4	4.5	16.7	1.4	1.2	0.1	19.4	431.1
1965-66	−18.1	10.7	28.8	2.6	12.1	14.7	9.7	15.4	1.0	1.5	0.1	18.0	185.6
1966-67	−0.2	5.2	5.4	2.6	8.1	10.7	19.7	18.2	2.1	2.8	0.1	23.2	117.8
1967-68	−5.1	13.9	19.0	3.8	8.8	12.6	6.3	21.4	1.6	3.8	0.2	27.0	428.6
1968-69	−3.5	3.1	9.6	1.5	11.5	13.0	13.4	21.0	2.2	3.5	0.1	26.8	200.0
1969-70	−12.5	10.0	22.5	1.2	5.4	6.6	8.2	23.8	3.0	2.3	0.1	29.2	122.7
Total	−37.3	59.7	97.0	13.9 (17.5)	66.1 (82.5)	80.0 (100.0)	61.8	116.5 (81.0)	11.4 (7.9)	15.1 (10.6)	0.8 (0.5)	143.8 (100.0)	232.7

Source : RBI Bulletin, June 1974 and July 1975.

*These figures relate to all foreign controlled rupee companies and not only to subsidiaries.

Figures in parenthesis in cols. 9, 10, 11 and 12 show their relative share of the amount in col, 13.

Figures in parenthesis in cols. 5 and 6 show their relative share of the amount in col. 7.

which, Rs. 13.9 crores only, was the investment in cash. If we take into account the practice of making up of machinery and components supplied by the parent company, the real contribution of the investment in kind to the balance of payment can easily be estimated to that extent. What is more, the remittance of profit accrued on that part of investment which was represented simply by price mark up, caused a perpetual loss of foreign exchange without any gain on that account. If the real effects caused on balance of payment by the transfer pricing, technology transfer, remittances and profit margins on what they have imported from the parent organisations the picture would be quite staggering. But the loss of such cannot be quantified on account of lack of exact information.

If we analyse the inflow of equity *vis-a-vis* the amount of profit, royalties and technical fees transmitted abroad the outcome is far from satisfactory. Between 1964-65 and 1969-70 the net inflow of funds into the subsidiaries by way of equity participation by the foreign partner amounted to Rs. 61.8 crores, while during the same period the remittance of dividends amounted to Rs. 116.5 crores, royalty payments to Rs. 11.4 crores, technical fee payments Rs. 15.1 crores and payments to foreign technicians in foreign currency came to Rs. 0.8 crores. In all, outpayments exceeded the equity investment by Rs. 82 crores. In some of the years the outflow was as high as 431.1 per cent of the net inflow. What is important is that dividends remittances accounted for more than 80 per cent of the total outpayments. Higher profit remittances contributed by higher profit generation and also by higher share of equity of parent organisation. At the same time higher magnitude of profits was attributed to higher profitability rates and re-investment of profits. Coca-Cola was sold to Indian public at a profit of 400 per cent.[9] A review of 34 foreign firms in drug industry showed that they earned 19.85 per cent profit on bulk drugs and 18.80 per cent on formula drugs in 1969-70.[10] However, on an average, the ratio of profits to the capital employed in the FCRCs during 1964-70 varied in the range of 11.2 per cent and 13.8 per cent[11] and reinvest-

9. The Economic Times, August 9, 1977.
10. The Economic Times, April 20, 1975.
11. RBI Bulletins, June 1968, p. 753 ; June 1973, p. 946 ; March 1971, p. 419 ; May 1972, p. 825 ; October 1973, p. 1653.

ment of profits between 38.6 per cent and 48.2 per cent of the profits earned making the capital base wider.

The ratio of profits remittances to the profit generated in the subsidiaries (net) was as large as 36.4 per cent during 1964-70.[12] The apparent reason was that the parent organisation held major shares in the equity. Among 537 FCRCs[13] 104 companies were having more than 25 per cent of foreign participation, 257 companies more than 40 per cent, 176 companies more than 50 per cent foreign participation. Though the government was never in favour of majority foreign participation and were rarely permitted. But they became frequent in the wake of foreign exchange crisis in late fifties and the government allowed foreign equity participation in lieu of plants and machinary and in some cases for the technology transferred. This provision was taken full advantage of and the parent organisation marked up their prices for getting larger share in equities. Glaxo, for example, started with the initial capital of Rs. 1.5 lakhs and widened its share upto Rs. 720 lakhs in the share capital (75 per cent of share capital). Low priority industries too were allowed. For example, Horlicks Ltd. with 83.3 per cent and Nestles Holdings Ltd. getting 90 per cent share in the equity capital,[14] though now reduced on account of FERA. But again most of the companies got stayed on the basis of section 29 on the pretext of sophisticated technology and export orientation. And thus no significant relief is in sight for near future.

THE TECHNOLOGY ISSUE

The technology issue now. 86 out of 197 subsidiaries[15] imported technology—patents, trade marks and know-how. In all there were 167 agreements. Of them 23 contracts had a life upto the completion of specific projects. In one contract equities were issued for technology and 18 agreements involved payments on continuing basis. Of the remaining 125, 11 had a life of more than 15 years, 13 between 10 and 15 years, 74 between 5 and 10 years and 27 below 5 years. From the view point of royalty, 109 cases were analysed. In 20 cases royalty payments were tagged

12. RBI Bulletin, June 1974.
13. RBI Bulletin, July 1975, p. 457.
14. Kust, M.J., "Foreign Enterprise in India : Laws and Policies," Oxford University Press, Bombay, 1964, p. 150.
15. RBI Bulletin, June 1974.

with either volume of profits or production. In others royalty was linked with the value of sales or production. Thus duration and rates of royalty payments were in most cases not favourable to India.

ENHANCING EXPORTS

The higher import bill of foreign companies would not have mattered much if sufficient exports would have been made. But the export of the subsidiaries during the period 1964-70 was hardly one-third of their imports.[16] In fact in this regaid the policy of parent organisation is more important. The general policy of mutinational corporations are to meet the local demands or in some cases secure raw meterial supplies.[17] Many agreements are associated with export restrictions to some specific countries or permission to some. In some cases permission was made a necessary provision for export of that product and so on. This has already been elaborated schemetically in the chapter entitled as Restrictive Business Practices and Transfer Pricing. This has naturally affected the balance of payments position of the host nations adversely.

During 1975-76 to 1977-78

The RBI has conducted its study[18] on 1,353 companies of which 276 were FCRCs. In terms of size, FCRCs accounted for about 35 per cent by paid-up capital and about 30 per cent each by total net assets and net sales of all 1,353 companies. Net sales per unit of total net assets were more or less around 1.25 for both the FCRCs and the Indian companies during the year 1977-78. The earnings in foreign exchange of FCRCs were Rs. 208.8 crores during 1975-76 which increased to Rs. 285.4 crores (36.7 per cent) in 1976-77 and remained at the level in 1977-78. Against this the outgo in foreign currency at Rs. 227.7 crores during 1975-76 increased to Rs. 288.5 crores in next two years. On an average for the three year period, the earnings in

16. RBI Bulletin, June 1974.
17. Allen, T.W., 'Direct Investment of European Enterprises in South East Asia', Economic Cooperation Centre for the Asian and Pacific Region, Bangkok, 1973. pp. 19-24.
18. RBI Bulletin, July 1981, pp. 560-611.

Table 5.5

Earnings and Outgo in Foreign Exchange—Indian Companies and FCRCs 1975-76 to 1977-78

(Rs. in lakhs)

	Indian Companies (1077)			FCRCs (276)		
	1975-76	1976-77	1977-78	1975-76	1976-77	1977-78
1. Paid-up Capital	1,111,43	1,188,57	1,232,07	564,93	605,08	659,08
2. Total Net Assets	6,726,63	7,102,33	7,629,46	2,701,65	2,910,17	3,191,37
3. Net Sales	7,711,87	8,610,90	9,488,05	3,403,64	3,852,80	4,057,25
4. RM & S Consumed	4,621,02	5,110,34	5,721,71	2,013,82	2,217,46	2,344,97
5. Profit after Tax	118,35	100,00	174,83	137,59	165,29	145,65
6. Dividends	87,94	98,02	109,53	70,45	84,95	89,29
7. Imported RM & S	419,80	493,98	807,63	256,85	309,41	364,09
8. Earnings in F/Exchange of which	471,33	631,52	651,79	208,80	285,43	284,64
(i) Exp. of goods	454,68	605,63	629,91	201,10	269,74	269,01
(ii) Royalty	69	14	22	65	60	55
(iii) Interest	56	1,13	84	49	52	54
(iv) Dividends	16	22	33	—	—	—
9. Outgo in Foreign Exchange of which	349,56	388,24	651,28	277,66	264,77	288,47
(i) Imports	317,34	340,60	607,57	191,43	212,80	234,12
(ii) Other Exp. in foreign currency	30,16	44,16	39,53	20,10	20,08	17,61
(iii) Dividends in FC	2,06	3,47	4,18	16,13	31,86	36,74
Percentages						
1. Imported to total RM & S consumed	9.1	9.7	14.1	12.8	14.0	15.5
2. Imports+Other Exp. in FC to Net Sales	4.5	4.5	6.8	6.2	6.0	6.2
3. Earnings in F/Exchange to Net Sales	6.1	7.3	6.9	6.1	7.4	7.0
4. Exp. in FC (excluding Dividend) to Earnings in Foreign Exchange	73.7	60.9	99.3	101.3	81.6	88.4
5. Dividend remitted in FC to PAT	1.7	3.5	2.5	11.7	19.3	25.2
6. Current Dividends remitted to PAT	—	0.1	—	0.3	2.4	4.3

Source : RBI. Bulletin, July 1981, p. 580.

foreign exchange of FCRCs were more or less off-set by the outgo in foreign currency. The performance of the Indian companies on the other hand was relatively good. The Indian companies earned foreign exchange to the tune of Rs. 471.3 crores in 1975-76. The earnings increased by 34 per cent to Rs. 631.5 crores in 1976-77 and further to Rs. 651.8 crores in 1977-78. The outgo in foreign currency which amounted to Rs. 349.6 crores in 1975-76 increased to Rs. 388.2 crores in 1976-77 and suddenly rose to Rs. 651.3 crores in 1977-78 by as much as 67.8 per cent. There was a surplus in foreign exchange by Indian companies amounting to Rs. 121.8 crores and Rs. 243.3 crores during 1975-76 and 1976-77 respectively. However, due to the substantial increase in the imports and very little increase in the exports of goods, the surplus of foreign exchange during 1977-78 was negligible. The average surplus was about Rs. 121.9 crores per year on the foreign exchange transactions of Indian companies.

The dividends remitted in foreign currency by the FCRCs were Rs. 16.1 crores, Rs. 31.9 crores, and Rs. 36.7 crores during 1975-76, 1976-77 and 1977-78 respectively. The ratio of the dividends remitted in foreign currency to profit after tax was 11.7 per cent in 1975-76 for FCRCs. It increased to 19.3 per cent and 25.2 per cent in the next two years. The situation can be seen from the Table 5.5.

The observation of the RBI study that "the reliance on imported raw materials and stores by FCRCs was higher as compared to that by the Indian companies" ... re-establishes the earlier point of higher import intensity of foreign companies and lower export performance index as has been discussed in Chapter 4.

THE RECENT DATA

Though the Indianisation process of foreign companies has begun and a great amount of criticism is being levelled against them, yet the outflow of funds continues unabated. It is really a matter of great interest to study the question that how far Indianisation has helped in checking the outflow of funds. Out of seven foreign companies chosen at random (namely, Flakt SF

Table 5.6

Total Inflow and Outflow of Funds of Seven Companies

Company	Years	Paid-up Capital	Imports	Exp. in FC	Earnings in FC	Dividends paid in foreign currency abroad
1. Flakt	1978	55,00,000	13,44,747	3,38,961	16,43,270	4,95,000
	1979	85,00,000	27,97,364	1,33,561	3,12,308	4,95,000
	1980	85,00,000	42,45,539	1,19,594	1,03,12,661	6,50,250
	1981	85,00,000	39,39,498	6,62,852	60,98,195	6,88,500
	1982	1,27,50,000	28,38,055	12,72,381	32,52,845	6,88,500
Total			1,51,65,203	25,27,379	2,16,19,279	30,17,250
		Total Outflow	2,07,09,832			
		Total Inflow	2,16,19,279			
		Balance	(+)9,09,447			
2. Ashok Leyland (Rs. in lakhs)	1979	16,50.04	11,00.47	68.89	5,05.85	100.21
	1980	16,50.04	21,33.66	71.38	6,17.28	156.59
	1981	16,50.04	31,17.44	1,95.64	7,45.66	75.16
	1982	16,50.04	20,05.27	2,61.26	28,43.35	75.16
Total			83,56.84	5,97.17	47,12.14	4,07.12
		Total Outflow	93,61.13			
		Total Inflow	47,12.14			
		Balance	(—)46,48.99			
3. Parke-Davis	1980	3,36,00,000	69,28,915	1,06,001	1,31,213	14,70,000
	1981	3,36,00,000	75,57,700	9,10,824	2,57,324	21,00,000
	1982	3,36,00,000	1,16,46,813	4,08,788	13,87,767	48,30,000
Total			2,61,33,428	14,25,613	17,76,304	84,00,000
		Total outflow	3,59,59,041			
		Total inflow	17,76,304			
		Balance	(—)3,42,22,737			

4. ITC Ltd. (Rs. in lakhs)					
1980	22,74	60,63	52,71	33,47,26	98,55
1981	27,29	1,61,20	77,34	35,57,48	1,02,00
1982	35,00	87,00	73,00	53,20,00	1,03,55
1983	35,00	3,20,00	94,00	72,60,00	1,46,87
Total		6,28,23	297,05	194,84,74	4,77,97
Total outflow	14,03,25				
Total inflow	194,84,74				
Balance	(+) 180,81,49				

5. Guest Keen Williams (Rs. in lakhs)					
1978	1,459.92	153.52	11.53	121.06	60.20
1979	1,459.92	478.23	25.50	438.52	77.38
1980	1,459.92	825.34	12.34	209.25	90.30
1981	1,459.92	1,151.03	19.76	209.52	90.34
1982	1,459.92	498.21	22.55	243.50	103.24
Total		3,103.33	91.68	1,221.86	421.46
Total outflow	3,619.47				
Total inflow	1,221.86				
Balance	(−) 2,397.61				

6. May and Baker					
1978	5,00,000	1,13,48,363	—	35,61,200	—
1979	1,80,16,050	1,05,75,958	15,860	14,15,958	—
1980	3,00,00,000	1,90,76,156	52,777	60,76,375	—
1981	3,00,00,000	1,53,61,001	1,01,166	37,88,831	65,29,740
1982	3,00,00,000	2,28,38,664	1,16,561	32,77,290	16,20,000
1983	4,50,00,000	2,19,58,670	2,60,392	16,78,724	18,90,000
Total		10,11,58,812	5,46,756	1,97,98,438	1,00,39,740
Total outflow	207,02,377				
Total inflow	197,98,438				
Balance	(−) 9,03,939				

(Contd.)

Table 5.6 (Contd.)

Company	Years	Paid-up capital	Imports	Exp. in FC	Earnings in FC	Dividends paid in foreign currency abroad
7. Firestone Rubber (now Modistone (Rs. 000's)	1978	33,300	12,250	491	8,506	—
	1979	45,000	16,499	207	1,826	—
	1980	45,000	19,596	116	576	—
	1981	45,000	25,282	36	46	—
	1982	45,000	26,635	131	—	—
	1983	45,000	33,6,87	404	4,685	—
Total			1,33,940	1,385	15,639	—

Total outflow   1,35,325
Total inflow   15,639
Balance   (—) 1,19,686

Source : Various Annual Reports of the Companies.

India Ltd., Ashok Leyland, ITC Ltd., Parke-Davis, Guest Keen Williams, May and Baker and Firestone Rubber) only two have reported to have contributed positively to the foreign exchange position. One of these two companies is mainly service company (ITC Ltd.) and, therefore, it is not surprise if it earns foreign exchange. But all manufacturing companies except one (Flakt) have negative impact on the balance of payments position. The facts can be verified from the Table 5.6.

CONCLUSIONS

The impact of MNCs on Indian balance of payments in general has been negative. Various outflows on account of dividend remittances, royalties, technical fees and payment to foreign technicians, import of raw material and spares in foreign currency have far exceeded the inflow on account of investment in cash and kind, exports, etc. On the other hand the Indian companies have fared better not only in terms of balance of payment but also in terms of their export performance and import intensity.

Lack of data on intra-firm trading (or transfer pricing), under-the-counter remittances in one way or the other have in no doubt exercised a drain on already meagre foreign exchange resources of the host developing countries. At the same time the developing nations are deprived of the benefits of international trade by their being oligopolistic in structure their vertical and horizontal integration, their inter-locking directorates and their cross-subsidisation of activities together with their massive access to financial resources. The dream of operation of new world economic order could perhaps not become true unless a serious thought is given to the significance and ramification of the multinational corporations in context of global economic system. By sheer idea of transferring their investment/assets from one country to another could place the host country's economy in jeopardy, especially of those which are small countries like that of Africa's and Latin America's.

UNCTAD Report, sub-titled as 'Dimensions of Corporate Marketing Structure has given a vivid picture about the dominating role of multinational corporations in world commodity trade shrinking the world trade as a whole and concentrating it in a few oligopolistic hands.

SUGGESTIONS

1. The developing countries should consider including provisions in their initial agreement with multinational corporations which permit the possibility of reduction over time of the percentage of foreign ownership ; the term as far as possible should also be agreed upon at the very beginning.

2. Before entering into any agreement the balance of payment implications of an MNC's activities must be given a serious thought. In case it appears to cause any negative impact on the balance of payments such foreign investments or technology should be discouraged, unless and otherwise required for serving the national interest.

3. Where ownership is an important objective for the host countries, consideration should be given to the establishment of joint venture as well as to the reduction over time of the share of foreign equity interests.

4. The host countries should explore alternative ways of importing technology other than by foreign direct investment, and should acquire the capacity to determine which technology would best suit their needs. Help may be solicited from international institutions if need be.

5. The home and host countries both should enforce arm's length pricing wherever appropriate ; and should elaborate rules on pricing practices for tax purposes. This will help doing away with the over-invoicing and under-invoicing problems and their probable impact on the balance of payments position.

REGULATION OF MULTINATIONAL CORPORATIONS

Introduction

The Choice

The Existing Regulatory System

Regional Efforts to Regulate the MNCs

Indian System of Regulation

Search for Regulatory Mechanism—Question of Nationality

Mechanism for Controlling the MNCs

Why MNC's Activities be Controlled

Nature of Control

Entities to be Covered

Means for Effective Implementation

National Entry Control System

NECS : The Relationship between LDCs and MNCs

Potential Implications of NECs

Indian Case—Companies Act, FERA

6

Regulation of Multinational Corporations

INTRODUCTION

The consideration of any kind of regulatory framework in the host countries' economies brings in the question of relationship between government and business (between MNCs and government), between government and government (between host and home countries). Complexities of present problem indicate that there are more than one questions involved here. There is the relationship between the home country's government and its enterprises operating transnationally, and symmetrically, the relationship between the host country's government and its domestic firms that may or may not be operating transnationally but are going to be affected if firms are allowed to come in. The latter relationship naturally tends to influence the relationship between the host country's government and the foreign firms. What should be the frame of reference that will help in disentangling the complexities ? A great question indeed. The framework should cover, to quote Gunnar Myrdal, "Two requirements ought to ensure that the technology of economies will not end up in traditional metaphysics ; first, it should always formulate its value premises explicitly in concrete terms and relate them to the actual valuations of social groups ; second, in formulating the relevant attitudes, the problem of social psychology should not be neglected."[1]

---

1. Myrdal, Gunnar, "The Political Element in the Development of Economic Theory", 1953, p. 204.

The value premises to be made explicit are concerned with the assertion that national approach is superior to any international approach in dealing with, and more specifically regulating the operations of multinational corporations. The value judgment involved here is that even for a country like India, which is fast developing the potential of capital outflow, far greater significance continues to be attached to the question of capital inflows. Now the major concern of a host country is not with the narrow BOP problems as affected by the capital inflows and the subsequent outflows on account of repatriations ; it is with the overall problem of capital formation including aspects like industry-wise composition and the pattern of ownership and financing. Consequently, in defining attitudes towards foreign firms a high degree of significance is attached to the impact they are going to have on the working of domestic firms including the 'imitation effect'.

THE CHOICE

Any control mechanism aiming to minimise or eliminate the adverse effects of the activities of the MNCs cannot be directed solely to one aspect of the activities to the exclusion of others. Nor can this control mechanism be of universally international character in a standardised form applicable to all MNCs irrespective of their size, character and importance to the political economies where they are operating and the needs and requirements of the development of the host countries. Further no international action in a mandatary form is feasible in the present international climate of sensitive nationalistic approach to international problems, which assume an acute form where transfer of resources from the rich to the poor, from developed to the under-developed, is involved. The realisation of these facts made the Group of Eminent persons to frame their recommendations for actions at the national level as well as at the international level.

In the first place the choice put forth is between a national system of regulation and an international system : and not between regulation and *laissez-faire*. The need for regulating the

economic processes in a market oriented economy is not in doubt.
But in the developing economies where large corporations in
their oligopolistic character exploit the imperfections of the
market and the foolproof regulation is all the more necessary
albeit difficult. The suggestion is that it is better done through
whatever system of control a particular nation considers worth-
while to have rather than through a universal code of discipline.
It is probable that for so large as we can conveniently foresee,
governments must insist on a high degree of sovereignty over
their economic affairs in order to provide a national economic
framework for the activities of their people on the one hand,
and on the other to ensure that the economic needs are represented as identifiable claimants for international consideration."[2]

It may even be asserted, without fear of contradiction, that
the only ideology in the world today is that of nationalism. The
old as well as the new nations enjoy the full freedom and, by
and large, have the full scope of determining their own economic
policies, and choosing their own options. This is a reality that
cannot be left unconsidered or done away with.

Nor are the international institutions to be wished away.
Their importance lies in their being the rallying points for nations
with common problems in specific contexts or as devices for re-
conciling conflicting interests of various nations. An apt illustration of this viewpoint is the recent developments in the sphere of
international monetary relations, general agreements on tariffs
and trade, United Nations Conference on Trade and Development
and even on non-economic issues like resolutions in security council meant for world peace and disarmament. On the contrary, the
range and the instruments of national intervention have got
widened. Even the Group of Eminent Persons could feel it while
expressing that "a code of conduct may be (merely) a consistent
set of recommendations which are gradually evolved and which
may be revised as experience or circumstances require. Although
they are not compulsory in character, they act as an instrument
of moral persuasion strengthened by the authority of international
organisation and the support of public opinion."[3]

---

2. Penrose, Edith, "The State and Multinational Enterprise" in John H.
   Dunning (ed.), "The Multinational Enterprise", 1971, pp. 238-39.
3. U.N., "The Impact of Multinational Corporations on Development and
   on International Relations," 1974, p. 55.

What is more as Vernon has argued, "...if some elaborate international regime should eventually emerge, it will not be because foreign investors were clamouring for it. More likely, it would arise out of a recognition on the part of governments that for one reason or another their interest demanded such a regime... (But for that) governments, particularly US government, would have to distinguish the national interests from the interests of their multinational enterprises more explicitly than they have in past."[4]

What about the argument that modern technology has rendered national boundaries obsolete ? Stephen Hymer and Rowthorn have very ably and effectively answered this question while stating "... (this argument) contains strong element of technological determinism and greatly oversimplifies and badly mistakes the trends."[5]

It may be worth reminding that regulation implies both promotion and restriction. The case is further strengthened if it is viewed in relation to the basic nature of cost-benefit calculus involved here. For a host country, as Reuber says, "the economic gains of foreign investments...are measured in terms of the value added to production less the opportunity cost of local factors used in production and after tax profit and dividends paid to the foreign investor."[6]

Thus in framing rules or a code of conduct for MNCs, one reality that cannot and should not be ignored is that the MNCs have come to stay as world entities emphasising the economic interdependence of the planet, and today they possess the tools for affecting the development process. The Declaration on International Development and Multinational Corporations of the OECD[7] draws attention to the fact that the MNCs could play an important role in the international investment process. This is

---

4. Vernon, R., "Future of the Multinational Enterprise" in C.P. Kindleberger (ed.), "The International Corporation," 1970, p. 395.
5. Hymer, Stephen and Rowthorn, Robert, "Multinational Corporations and International Oligopoly" in C.P. Kindleberger (ed.) *op. cit.*, p. 87.
6. Reuber, Grant L., *et. al.*, "Private Foreign Investment in Development," 1973, p. 17.
7. OECD, Declaration on "International Investment and Multinational Enterprises" Press Release, A(76) 20, 21 June 1976.

echoed by the Pacific Basin Charter on International investment.[8] In the Lome Convention, in article 26 on Industrial Corporation, one of the objectives stated is to encourage community firms to participate in the industrial development of the member States.[9]

THE EXISTING REGULATORY SYSTEM

There have been efforts both at the international and national level to regulate and control the activities of the MNCs. Some of the international conventions have also deliberated in detail on this issue. Efforts for thrashing out the issues conceptually and functionally have been made by India and Columbia by defining the MNCs in their respective legal framework (as given in Chapter 1).

The ANDEAN Foreign Investment Code (Decision 24) also emphasises that foreign capital can make a considerable contribution in the economic development of Latin America provided it stimulates capital formation in the country where it is established.[10] National regulations are there in the developed and developing countries dealing with foreign investment but no developed or developing country has yet enacted a comprehensive regulation for dealing with MNCs in a single comprehensive instrument. Various aspects of their activities are dealt with in fragmented pieces of legislation. Anti-trust legislations are there in the USA...in the form of the Sherman Anti-trust Act (1890) ; The Clayton Act (1914) ; The Federal Trade Commission Act (1914) and the Webb-Pomerene Act (1918) ; in UK in the form of MRTP Act (on the lines of which Indian MRTP Act was formulated), in Germany, Anti-Trust Act 1957 ; in India MRTP Act 1970, FERA 1973 etc. etc.

Apart from the absence of any specific legislation on the activities of the MNCs existence of un-coordinated enactments dealing with specific machinery to administer these enactments

---

8. Pacific Basin Economic Council, The Pacific Basin Charter on "International Investment : A Declaration of Basic Principles" adopted on May 19, 1972.
9. ACP, EEC Convention of Lome, 28 February 1973, Article 26(g).
10. Commission of the Cartigena Agreement, "Common Regime of Treatment of Foreign Capital and of Trade Marks, Patents, Licences and Royalties," para 2.

have tended to create a certain amount of uncertainty about the rights, duties and obligations of these corporations. They have also placed the concerned governments in a weak position while taking a total view in regard to screening and admission of these corporations for entry into the economic process of the country. There is no uniformity in the matter of submission of disputes arising from agreements with foreign enterprises. In some cases the agreements refer to municipal law and the domestic tribunals as the proper forum. In some other cases, the disputes are resolved in accordance with international law by court outside the jurisdiction of home and the host countries. In some other cases, the disputes are to be resolved in accordance with the collaborators' law and in foreign courts.

REGIONAL EFFORTS TO REGULATE THE MNCs

At the regional level, two significant developments have been made in regard to the formulation of norms for controlling the activities of various enterprises though even here there is no specific code or set of rules applicable solely to the MNCs. The leading example of the regional attempt to have an agreement among member countries for limiting the influence of foreign capital is that of the ANDEAN Foreign Investment Code (Decision 24) made under the Cartigena Agreement of 1968. Under this agreement the member countries[11] restricted the total foreign ownership in enterprises within the sub-region and laid down a rule for majority participation by Latin American countries in any joint ventures with foreigners. Rules have also been framed for repatriation of funds by foreign companies and for disinvestment of foreign companies where national skills and investment have developed. So far this is the only agreement on regional basis having a common Code for, the establishment and regulation of activities of foreign enterprises. There have been attempts for forming similar groupings, for example by ASEAN countries to achieve a common trade and investment policies, but no concrete results have emerged so far. The European Economic Community made some useful attempts in evolving a European Common Laws which may possibly, if successfully implemented, prove effective in

---

11. Peru, Columbia, Bolivia, Equador, Venezuela (Chile Withdrew in Oct. 1976).

harmonisation of the company law regulations within the community.

Among other regional agreements, for the purpose of forming free trade areas is the East African Community set up in 1967 to regulate the industrial and commercial relations among the three countries of the region providing, among other things, for a Common Commercial Law for regionally owned corporations.

A specific formulation for MNCs on a regional basis is the well known as OECD, laying down specific guidelines for regulating the conduct of multinational corporations and the policies to be adopted by the member countries for these MNCs. These guidelines deal with the problems that arise from the study of the impact of MNCs activities, suggesting to adopt the general policies by the MNCs such as giving due consideration to the member countries' objectives and priorities, favouring close co-operation with the local community, refraining from corrupt practices and abstaining from involving in local political processes. Specific provisions have also been included to pay respect to BOP and Credit policies, avoiding restrictive trade practices, furnishing necessary information to the revenue authorities, avoiding transfer pricing for taking the advantage of lower tax liability, observance of constructive attitude towards employment generation and industrial relations and fitting their operations within the scientific and technological capacities and framework.

INTERNATIONAL EFFORTS TO REGULATE MNCs

At the international level, there has been as yet no instrument dealing with the affairs of MNCs. The maiden effort in this direction started with the report from the Group of Eminent Persons—Impact of MNCs on Development and International Relations. However, attempts have been made at the international level, even before the resolutions of the Economic and Social Council at its fifty seventh session, to deal with the matter relating to the activities of the MNCs and private foreign investment. In 1948, the UN considered international investment and restrictive trade practices, as reflected in Article 12 and

46-54 of the Hawana Charter.[12] The principle of permanent
national sovereignty over natural resources have been the subject
matter of many General Assembly resolutions.[13]

The UNCTAD Conference at its second session in 1968 (held
at New Delhi), called for a work programme on restrictive business practices and for a study of the issues on flow of private
capital to developing countries. The issue of transfer of technology to LDCs also received special attention. Various General
Assembly resolutions (1713-*xvi*) and Economic and Social Council
resolution (834-*xxxiii*), the Department of Economic and Social
Affaris of the UN examined in 1961 various aspects of the
problem. In 1970, the UNCTAD initiated a programme of work
for revision of international patent system and for framing a
code of conduct for transfer of technology. The harmonisation
of tax problems by undertaking necessary studies on tax treaties
has been carried out right since 1968 by an Expert Group,
assisted by the UN Department of Economic and Social Affairs.

In considering these problems, the related questions of transfer pricing and tax evasion have also been examined. Following
the adoption of resolution (UN resolution No. 2918-*xxvii*) the
United Nations Commission on International Trade and Law
(UNCITRAL) has taken up the legal questions related to MNCs
and international law. But no code has been formulated, may be
for want of proper code of conduct to be formulated by the UN
Commission on Transnational Corporations which would then be
considered for formulating the appropriate legal instrument.
Furthermore, the regional studies have also been made, though
on a limited scale, by the ESCAP, the Economic Commission for
Latin America, the Economic Commission for Africa on problems
related to the impact of MNCs on their respective regions as a
whole, and on certain countries or industries. The World Bank
in 1965, started an International Centre for Settlement of
Investment Disputes providing facilities for conciliation and
arbitration of any legal disputes arising directly out of an

12. See UN Document, Sales No. 1948 III D. 4 ; The UN Conference on
    Trade and Employment held at Hawana from 21-24 March 1948, Final
    Act and Related Documents.
13. Resolutions No. 626 (vii), 1803 (xvii), 2158 (xxi), 2386 (xxiii), 2692 (xxv),
    3016 (xxvii), 3171 (xxviii), 3175 (xxviii).

investment between a contracting State and a national of another State.[14] If it is accepted by all the members of the World Bank, it would be a significant advancement in the settlement of disputes.[15]

INDIAN SYSTEM OF REGULATION

In India also there is no system of regulation which deals exclusively with the activities of multinational corporations. Like others, India too, have fragmented piece of legislation dealing with some specific activities of foreign companies as well as domestic firms. For example, the Companies Act, 1956 deals only with the rules to be observed by the foreign company.[16] The Foreign Exchange Regulation Act, 1973 is concerned with the matters relating to equity and loan arrangements by foreign companies in India and use of foreign trade marks and patents.[17] In the same manner, the Foreign Money Contribution Act Prohibits contribution by foreign companies ; the Industrial Development and Regulation Act, 1951 deals with licensing for establishing a business in scheduled industries ; the control of Capital Issues Act, 1947 relates to the issue of capital and conversion of Companies' share capital ; the MRTP Act, 1969 details the regulation for curbing the concentration of economic power by industrial undertakings (Sections 20-26) ; the Patent and Designs Act, 1970 provides for registration of patents including patents of foreign companies ; the Trademarks and Merchandise Act, 1958 deals with registration of trademarks. From this list of various legislations, except FERA and Foreign Contribution Act, all other are common to foreign and domestic enterprises. The Foreign Contribution Act alone has a definition of multinational corporation for the purpose of placing a ban on such corporations' financing persons, or individuals or bodies for prevention of corrupt practices.[18]

---

14. UN Doc. E/C. 10/18 "Transnational Corporations : Material Relevant to Formulation of Code of Conduct," New York, 1974, para 271, p. 79.

15. For further discussion see Salzmary, Herbert ; "Political Risks of Investment in Less Developed Countries" in George W. Ball, (ed.) 'Global Companies', Prentice Hall, New Jersey, 1975, pp. 95-96.

16. Section 591 of the Companies Act, 1956.

17. Sections 28 and 29 of the FERA 1973.

18. See for definition Chapter 1.

In India, according to information furnished by 44 public undertakings to the Parliamentary Committee on Public Undertakings, in 19 out of 74 foreign collaboration agreements, the venue of arbitration has been outside the country.[19] In another 19 cases, the law applicable for arbitration was the Indian Arbitration Act, while in 36 cases it was International Chamber of Commerce Regulations, and in 5 cases was the law of Collaborators' country.[20] In view of the conflicting regulations, it is necessary to explore, at least in a broad outline, in what manner the national regulations must be framed with a view to achieving the objectives of minimising the abuses and controlling the conduct of MNCs to fall in line with the host countries' socio-political economic goals of their society.

SEARCH FOR REGULATORY MECHANISM—QUESTION OF 'NATIONALITY'

Among the various obstacles faced in the way of formulating the legislative instrument dealing with the multinational corporations the biggest obstacle was settling the question of 'nationality' of the international corporation. While formulating any rules for control and regulation, an identification of the nationality of the corporation is necessary because one, it is the home State of the corporation which can issue certain prescriptive rules governing the conduct of the corporation and two, more importantly, when questions of diplomatic protection is to be accorded under the international law arise, the right of diplomatic protection is given only to the home State in respect of its nationals by taking up the case of one of its subjects.[21]

---

19. India, Fifth Lok Sabha, Committee on Public Undertakings (1975-76) 89th Report on Foreign Collaboration in Public Undertakings, New Delhi, 1976, Para 9.3, p. 261.
20. *Ibid.*
21. According to the Permanent Court of International Justice..."the rule of international law...is that in taking up the case of one of its nationals... a State is in reality asserting its own right, the right to ensure in the person of its nationals respect for the rules of international law. This right is necessarily to limit interventions on behalf of its own nationals because, in the absence of a special agreement, it is the bond of nationality between the State and the individual which alone confers upon the State the right of diplomatic protection, and it is as a part of the function of diplomatic protection that the right to take up a claim and to ensure respect for the rules of international law must be envisaged..."
    —Case of the Panevezya...Saldutiskis Ry., PCIJ, Series AB, No. 76, 16 (1939).

Transnational Corporations should primarily be the subject to national laws and not the international laws. But care has to be taken for not becoming the national laws an extra-territorial in its jurisdiction as happened in various cases relating to Sherman Act and Clayton Act of the USA. Even if mandatory terms are used in an international convention, or any resolution passed by the General Assembly, saying that the MNCs shall or shall not do a specified act, the implication of such a provision is that all the member States would take adequate action through their national laws for compliance by the MNCs. Having regard to these factors, the question of nationality assumes importance and it is pretty serious that this question has not appeared as an issue in the discussions relating to the formulation of any code of conduct held so far by the Commission on Transnational Corporations. The question of nationality has been well brought out by the reactions to the judgment of the International Court of Justice in Barcelona Traction Light and Power Company Ltd. (a Canadian firm) case.[22]

The issue of nationality arose when the International Court of Justice gave its verdict on the Barcelona Traction case caused by the non transfer of servicing payments on its bonds from Spain due to non-authorisation of payments abroad due to break out of civil war in Spain. Then added the Belgian claim for its nationals' interest in the company gave it a new dimension. First notable reaction to the decision came from Feliciano in 1966 when he presented a paper to the Academy of International Law on Legal Problems of Private International Business Enterprises[23] after the first phase judgment was delivered in 1964. A strong note of protest came as an editorial comment appeared in the American Journal of International Law.[24] By ruling that only the country of nationality of the shareholders, had *jus standi* to prefer claims

---

22. ICJ Reports (Second Phase) 1970.

23. Feliciano, Florentino P., "Legal Problem of Private International Business Enterprises : An Introduction" to the International Law of Private Business Association and Economic Law, Leyden, 1966.

24. "Two perspectives on the Barcelona Traction Case : The Rigidity of Barcelona", American Journal of International Law, Vol. 65, 1971, pp. 522-41.

in respect of any international injury inflicted on the Corporation. The International Court, it was argued, ignored the reality of corporate investment in modern world. The modern world corporations have their headquarters in one jurisdiction with stockholders drawn from more than one country with operations carried on in a third country through a branch or subsidiary created under the laws of the State. The case of Nestles is a leading example of such type. Nestles as is generally believed a Swiss Company, which it substantially is, but not legally, it is a company with its headquarters in Nassau, Bahamas, which is a tax haven. Though the bulk of the stock is held by Swiss, Nestles is operating in most of the third world nations and has subsidiaries in several or these countries. On the basis of the decision in case of Barcelona traction, if there is a branch of obligation in international law in a country where Nestles is operating through a subsidiary and if the State of incorporation, namely, Bahamas, refuses to afford diplomatic protection, the Swiss government, whose nationals are the real and substantial stockholders would be without competence to afford diplomatic protection unless it is proved that the injury has affected directly the rights of shareholders as such.[25]

There are various standards of nationality of a corporation. One, the place of incorporation is the generally favoured test in the common law countries and two, the siege social is the accepted test in the civil law system.[26] The control test was used to determine the character of property during war but has not been established as a general test of nationality for international corporation.[27] The 'genuine link' concept of nationality owes its origin to the judgment of Nottbohm case.[28] The genuine link-theory permits lifting of the Corporate Veil to find out the effective link between the corporations as an association of stockholders and the nation States. Of the four tests, the control and link tests have not, it is submitted, been developed into definite

25. ICJ Report, pp. 32-33.

26. Kronstein, "The Nationality of the International Enterprises", Columbia Law Review, 983 1952).

27. Observation of the PCIJ on the Control Test in Certain German Interests in Polish Upper Silesia", Series A, No. 7, p. 70.

28. ICJ Reports, 1955.

rules of international law relating to nationality and the link test was used by Justice Jessup only to pierce through the "Corporate Veil" to afford locus standi to the Belgian shareholders of the Barcelona Traction case. Thus tests of nationality narrow down only to "place of incorporation" or "siege social". The practice of States, as reflected in the bilateral treaties on friendship, commerce and navigation is to regard as national companies, those which are incorporated in these States.[29] The convention concerning recognition of legal personality of foreign companies, associations and foundations, drafted by the Seventh Hague Conference on Private International Law in 1951, provides for recognition, as a matter of right, by each contracting State of the legal personality acquired by a company established under the law of another contracting State. The treaty establishing the EEC speaks of companies constituted in accordance with the law of a particular State. Justice Moore in his Digest of International Law[30] remarks that it is well settled that a government may intervene on behalf of a company incorporated under its laws. The incorporation theory has also been accepted by the International Court of Justice. This happened in the Interhandel case.[31] This case along with the Barcelona case has established the rule of nationality on the basis of incorporation.

MECHANISM FOR CONTROLLING THE MNCs

There has been a great debate over the issue that what should be the mechanism of controlling the MNCs' activities. In fact it is not the MNCs which are to be controlled but their activities which have an adverse impact on the economies of the host countries.

WHY MNC's ACTIVITIES BE CONTROLLED

Though the various arguments have already been advanced in respective chapters to control the activities of the MNCs in

---

29. For instance the US Treaty with Iran (1955) and UK-Egypt Agreement of 1959.
30. Vol. 6, p. 641.
31. Interhandel Case, ICJ Report, 1959, p. 6.

the host countries but here also the arguments may be repeated briefly as—[32]

(*a*) much of the foreign direct investment going to the LDCs are based on capital intensive techniques whereas the economic conditions of these countries dictate the adoption of labour intensive processes. Furthermore, an inappropriate technology can make the recipient worse off ;

(*b*) due to international trade barriers instituted mainly by developed countries, and often for the protection of their own industries, LDCs have had difficulties in exporting manufactured goods and obtaining much needed hard currencies ;

(*c*) for a selected group of LDCs, it has been shown that MNCs' presence has had negative impact on their BOP as well as social incomes ;

(*d*) MNCs have, in general, manipulated both import and export prices through their intra-firm transfer pricing policies so that their activities have hurt attempts made for improving balance of payments problem ;

(*e*) employment benefits of MNCs' operations have been less than expected and at the same time distorted the labour market in LDCs ; and

---

32. These arguments have been framed after having consulted the following studies in particular :
   (*a*) "International Trade and the Developing Countries", American Economic Review, Vol. 68 ,1978, p. 264 ;
   (*b*) Cohen, B.I., "Alternative Theoritical Approach to the Impact of Foreign Investment on the Host Country," New Haven : Yale Econ. Growth Centre, Discussion Paper No. 164, 1972 ;
   (*c*) Muller, R., "Poverty is the Product in Transnational Corporations and World Order" by Modelski, G. (ed.), San Francisco, Freeman, 1979 ;
   (*d*) Muller, R.D. and Morgenstern, R.D., "Multinational Companies and Balance of Payments in LDCs : An Econometric Analysis of Export Pricing Behaviour", Kyklos, Vol. 27, 1974 ;
   (*e*) Nayyar, D., "Transnational Corporations and Manufactured Exports from Poor Countries", Economic Journal, Vol. 88, March 1978 ;
   (*f*) UN, "The Growth of the Pharmaceutical Industry in Developing Countries—Problems and Prospects," New York, 1978 ;
   (*g*) Helleiner, G.K., "Manufactured Exports from Less—Developed Countries and Multinational Firms", Economic Journal, Vol. 83, March 1973 ; and
   (*h*) Morawetz, D., "Employment Implications of Industrialisation in Developing Countries," Economic Journal, Vol. 84, September 1974.

(*f*) rising economic (and political) nationalism in many LDCs, increasing scepticism towards MNCs' activities and the subsequent desire (and demand) by the third world nations to have a greater degree of control over the agreements and contracts with MNCs have ultimately emerged.

Following points should be given thought when any mechanism to control the MNCs' activities is considered to be formulated :

(*a*) Nature of Control,

(*b*) Entities to be Covered,

(*c*) Means for Effective Implementation.

(*a*) **Nature of Control**

Two important questions have to be considered here. One, whether the control should be legislative or voluntary and two, whether it should be formulated at the national level or at the international level in the form of Code of Conduct as attempted by the UN. It has already been made clear that the primary concern of the MNCs' activities is national and this would imply regulations at the national level. Though the international level instruments (of course not in terms of legal binding) are there but they should be supplementary to the national legislative regulations. Also the fragmented pieces of regulations are not going to deliver the goods but a comprehensive enactment should be there instead of many acts.

(*b*) **Entities to be Covered**

It has to be considered whether the control should apply to only private MNCs or to State owned MNCs also. At the same time whether the regulation to be applied to all types of activities like manufacturing, trading or servicing or to the specific type of activities.

It may be submitted that control should not be confined only to private or one type of activities but to all MNCs, including the State owned. For, it is incorrect to imagine that an invest-

ment or collaboration from a State owned firm will behave only
in the interest of the host country. Because all of these are
strictly business agreements whose motive cannot be other than
profit or other political and economic influence from it. The
same amount of repatriation occur in case of USSR collaboration
as in the case of Western European collaborations—may be
under different nomenclatures. For example IDPL (a public
undertaking) having Russian Collaboration has experienced same
type of difficulties as others do.[33] The presence of foreign government entity in the form of a commercial concern is capable of
same political interference as has been found in the case of
private corporations.[34] In fact the situation may be even worse
because an independent corporation could resist moves of the
home government to use it as a tool of its foreign policy. But
there is no barrier of such resistance when the government agency
itself is operating within a foreign jurisdiction. It is, therefore,
suggested that any regulation in relation to the MNCs should
take in its umbrella all foreign corporations irrespective of their
ownership. This view is all the more strengthened when the State
owned and co-operative organisations have been included in the
definition of the MNC. If they become MNC, by definitions, then
why not such regulation be applied to them also.

At the same time all MNCs working in different sectors—
primary, secondary or tertiary—should be treated alike under
these national regulations. Though they may differ in
their impact on host countries' economies in terms of time and
intensity. Here the adequate consideration should be given to
the vertical and horizontal integration of these multinational
corporations. Further, in this time of technological innovations
they can easily diversify their activities. For example, Indian
Tobacco, which started as cigarettes manufacturer has fanned out

---

33. IDPL's complaint against USSR was that Performance guarantee
    offered was for 18 months from the date of receipt of last component,
    regardless of actual commissioning of the complete plant. IDPL felt
    that performance guarantee should be for 12 months from the actual
    commissioning. Secondly, the difficulties were experienced in trans-
    porting the plant as far as to include expenses/claims for losses or
    shortages since the suppliers did not agree to have a class of liquidated
    damages—the safeguard . . . against late delivery in India.

34. See Chapter II.

into hotel and engineering industry. Union Carbide, originally started as dry battery cell manufacturer is now engaged with the production of pesticides, marine fishing and export of garments. Another relevant question is whether the regulation should cover both host and parent countries while dealing with the MNCs. In consideration of this question, it should be borne into mind that the MNCs are qualitatively different entities from nation States as participants in international relations. In legal terms these corporations owe their creation to a national law and operate under laws of the country where they carry on their activities. They are just nationals of a State and are not subjects of international law, whereas States are sovereign entities which subject to the international law.

(c) Means for Effective Implimentation

Another very important question is how to enforce the existing mechanism and what new form of control mechanism be evolved. It may be recalled that the various forms and instruments used in the UN practices are treaties, conventions, protocols, agreements, declarations and resolutions. But the main problem is that convention, declarations have no legal binding on the countries and become non-functional in practice.

Following directive principles should be considered while formulating and executing the national regulation :

(a) the MNCs should function within the socio-economic framework of the country, and must be within the national priority of the host countries ;

(b) the host country must have the right to regulate the MNCs under their national laws. In case of any conflict between national and international law the former should prevail ;

(c) the MNCs must refrain from any involvement in the political process, directly or indirectly and must honour the human rights by not indulging in supporting the racist regimes. In such cases the MNCs should be asked to quit ;

(d) the MNCs should not indulge in corrupt practices including bribery or payment of money to parties and individuals under the dubious name of political contributions or donations ;

(*e*) the MNCs should not indulge in restrictive business practices (RBPs) which would have an adverse effect on the world trade and prevent countries from getting the benefits of competition ;

(*f*) transfer pricing should not be allowed in any case so as to underprice or overprice the intra-firm transactions so as to save tax ;

(*g*) reasonable price of transfer of technology must be ensured by an appropriate body on the basis of cost-benefit studies and the MNCs should be asked to establish research facilities in the host countries not in parent countries ;

(*h*) MNCs should be allowed only in the sectors and in those lines of products where indigenous capabilities are not available. What can be produced domestically should not be opened for MNCs ;

(*i*) those MNCs should be encouraged which have high export potentiality and less import intensities ;

(*j*) Repatriation of profits, technical fee and royalties should be made in such a manner that substantial proportion thereof should be re-invested in the host countries.

NATIONAL ENTRY CONTROL SYSTEM

Although individual and diverse laws on FDI inflows have been in existence in a few LDCs (for example in Mexico) for a number of years[35] many of these nations have confronted MNCs with their respective collective of FDI regulations being administered by the government agency or agencies. For our purpose here, we will prefer the name 'National Entry Control System' (NECS) to mean a collection of certain regulations directed at both entry and operational phases of various MNCs' projects.[36]

---

35. "How some Latin American countries deal with international Companies"—Business International, May 9, 1975 ; Robinson, R.D., "National Control of Foreign Business Entry," Praeger, New York, 1976 and various issues of Business International, Business Asia and Business Latin America.

36. Robinson was the first writer to refer to a collection of FDI regulations as an entry control system, *op. cit.*

The existing entry control systems of a number of LDCs (as well as developed countries) were studied in order to permit us to obtain all the essential details and also identify any common policies among various NECS. The results indicate that for a majority of the surveyed countries—especially the LDCs— the respective NECS contain several distinct elements, with each element directed at a specific characteristics of foreign investment. Furthermore, a comparison of various NECS shows the the existence of a number of common elements though with differing details and specifications.[37]

Table 6.1 presents a list of common elements in most of the surveyed countries. While "approval and registration" serves as the prerequisite to each NECS—permitting host countries to screen and admit only those desired foreign investment—each of the eight elements is being directed of a specific characteristic of foreign investment inflows.

Table 6.1
Common elements of the selected NECS Approval and Registration

1. Sectors	:	Directing more FDI inflows to priority economic activities.
2. Geography	:	Placing greater amounts of FDI in desired geographical location of a host country.
3. Ownership	:	Achieving more local ownership of foreign investments.
4. Acquisition	:	Regulating the number of local firms being acquired by MNCs.
5. Content	:	Requiring a given level of local contents in FDI based production.
6. Export	:	Requiring a given level of exports of MNCs/FDI based output.
7. Employment	:	Regulating the number of foreign employees at various levels of employment of each project.
8. Repatriation	:	Restricting Repatriation of profits and capital.

---

37. The entry system studied included those of Columbia, Brazil, Argentina, Maxico, Venezuela, India, Indonesia, Malaysia, Philippines, Thailand, Portugal, Yugoslavia, Algeria, Kenya, Canada, Belgium, Denmark, West Germany, Norway, UK, Australia and Japan etc.

NECS : THE RELATIONSHIP BETWEEN LDCs AND MNCs

Presently there are three different views prevailing on relationship between the LDCs and MNCs, each of which represents some widely held opinions.[38]

(a) *The Soverignty-at-bay Model* : Represents the 'liberalist' school of thought on political economy, the basic position of this model is that MNCs are the best allocators of global resources. The MNC is said to have the flexibility, resources, and the mobility which, if confronted with nationalistic demands of an LDC allow it to move its facilities and FDI elsewhere, thus causing that LDC to be the loser in terms of employment, technology and access to world markets.

(b) *The Dependencia Model* : It represents the 'Marxian' school of thought, the flow of wealth is seen as moving—via the MNCs—from the global, under-developed periphery to the centres of industrial financial power. This model considers development and under-development as simultaneous processes, maintaining that developed countries have grown rich through exploiting the poor and making them poorer. This seems to be more realistic on the basis of certain empirical facts as provided in foregoing chapters.

(c) *The Mercantilist Model* : This model is the representative of the 'economic nationalism' school of thonght, regards the nation State and the interplay of national interests—as distinct from corporate interests—as the primary determinants of the future conditions of the world economy. National governments are seen as manipulating economic arrangements in order to maximise their own interests. The model maintains that a new international economic and political order less favourable to the MNC is emerging.

The view advanced here, reflecting the existence of NECS, is predictive of an emerging relationship based, more than before,

---

38. The views are adapted from Gilpin in G. Modelski's (ed.) "Transnational Corporations and World Order," San Francisco : Freeman 1979. Also Hymer, S., "The Multinational Corporations A Redical Approach" (ed.) by Cohen, R.B. *et. al.*, New York, Cambridge University Press, 1979.

on the needs and desires of the host countries. Specifically, the view has following features :

(*a*) The number of NEC adopting countries is increasing regarding the relationship between LDCs and MNCs.

(*b*) Economic nationalism as reflected from the adoption of the NECs is becoming beneficial to developing countries. Because all the things become clear to coming MNCs and therefore, shading latent dangers in the host countries what the MNCs would face during their activities (But this aspect will depend not only on mere existence of NECS but by overall political environment of the host country).

(*c*) It has been shown that only some elements (as listed in Table 6.1) will have significant impact on host countries' economy—indeed based on both the degree of monitoring success for each element and potential economic impacts. The four elements are likely to play major roles as various LDCs attempt to achieve more benefits from the MNCs' investments : geographical location of MNCs ; priority economic sectors ; local contents in MNC backed projects ; exports of MNCs based output.

(*d*) Given the existence of NECS, one measure of MNC's response is the flow of investment. But somewhere it is seen that it is not the NEC but other variables like GNP, population, raw materials, etc., account for variations in investment flows and NECS playing insignificant role.[39]

(*e*) MNCs will respond to both incentives and restrictions in a manner which reflects their own economic 'welfare.' Two factors can influence this response. First, host developing countries are witnessing increasing competition among the MNCs based in different countries. As the LDCs diversify their source countries,

---

39. Hufbauer, G., "The Multinational Corporation and Direct Investment" in Kenen, P. (ed.) "International Trade and Finance," Cambridge University Press, London, 1975 ; Korbin, S., "The Environmental Determinants of Foreign Direct Manufacturing Investment—An Ex-post Empirical Analysis," Journal of International Business Studies, Fall Winter, 1976, Agodo, O., "The Determinants of US Private Manufacturing Investments in Africa," Journal of International Business Studies, Winter, 1978.

increasing competition for markets among various MNCs may be expected to lead to more compliance of the NECS. Second, the 'degree of restrictiveness' as well as the speed with host developing countries have adopted FDI regulations can negatively influence the MNC's response.

Overall the NECS-based approach to the relationship between LDCs and MNCs will be governed by certain economic and political factors. Although MNCs will continue to base their foreign investment decisions mainly on economic considerations, more local, rather than global, factors will have to be considered.

POTENTIAL IMPLICATIONS OF NECS

The global approach pursued by many MNCs has the following basic strategies—

(a) Plants and operations are situated worldwide in order to serve both local and foreign markets.

(b) Intra-firm transfers take place between various subsidiaries.

(c) Decisions are made mainly at the parent level covering global profit maximisation, market positions and overall growth.

With the emergence of economic nationalism – reflected in NECS—the operationg relationship between host developing countries and the multinationals has undergone certain changes. In order to examine the possible impacts of NECS on various characteristics of FDI and technical collaboration can be summarised as follows :

(a) Based on the rate and degree of responses provided by host governments, it seems that very few of those countries adopting NECS have indeed compiled an adequate data base necessary for mointoring MNC's compliance and for measuring the overall effectiveness of NECS. This may result in the lack of enforcement of entry control system.

(b) Monitoring results reveal that both across and within countries different degrees of success can be observed for different elements of NECS, with the four elements mentioned earlier having the most favourable outcomes. Evidence indicates that as specific sectors of an economy become further developed there is all likelihood for all elements of NECS to become effective and bring about desired changes in MNCs based FDI and collaborations' agreements.

(c) Element No. 3 (ownership) is found to be rather ineffective. The fact is that MNCS can establish inside host nations 'front' companies which, while in compliance with local ownership requirements, do not usually lead to local control of MNCs' projects. Element No. 4 (Acquisitions) is in fact unnecessary (theoretically) since funds released through MNC's acquisitions of local firms can potentially be put back into the economy to enhance local competition and employment.[40]

In sum, it is more important to note that as LDCs achieve further economic advancement, they will be in a better position to possess effective entry control systems which can lead to more positive contributions from the multinationals. Of course, one expects to see conflicts as each side attempts to exert and maintain more power in its relationship with the other side.

INDIAN CASE

In India there are multiplicity of regulations dealing with the activities of industrial and commercial enterprises both foreign and domestic alike. There is a case for separate legislation for dealing with the MNCs in India on the lines of Companies Act and MRTP Act. Until the separate legislation is enacted the existing ones should be suitably amended to give more teeths to deal with the MNCs.

The present position with regard to foreign companies in the Companies Act is the following :

(a) they are not companies within the meaning of the Act and the provisions of the Act would not, in general, apply to them unless any section in the Act either specifically refers to a foreign company or refers generally to bodies corporate ;

---

40. Behrman, Jack N., "National Interest and the Multinational Enterprirses—Tensions among the North, Atlantic Countries," Prentice Hall Inc., Englewood Cliffs, New Jersey, 1970, p. 138.

(*b*) in some of the sections of the Act, the provisions have been made specifically applicable to foreign companies, *e.g.*, sub-section (2) (b) of Section 202 ;

(*c*) some sections of the Act apply to foreign companies because of the use of the expression 'body corporate' in those sections, *e.g.*, sections 4, 42, 43A, 370, 372, etc. ;

(*d*) by the amendment Act of 1974, a new clause, *viz.*, Clause (b) of sub-section (3) of Section 600 has been added and by virtue of this clause, sections 159, 209, 209A, 233A, 233B, and 234 to 246 have been made applicable to foreign companies ;

(*e*) the specific provisions which are applicable to a foreign company are incorporated in a separate part, namely, Part XI, that appears in the present Act in Sections 591 and 602.

(*f*) a new sub-section namely, sub-section (2) of section 591 has been added by the Amendment Act 1974 by which a new class of foreign companies namely, 'deemed companies,' has been created.

According to the Sacher Committee[41] the present position regarding the foreign companies is quite unsatisfactory. "We are particularly against the practice of first allowing certain bodies corporate incorporate outside India to be registered as foreign companies and then apply a large number of sections in the Act, not otherwise applicable to them by making indirect provisions here and there and from time to time. Instead, it would be desirable to lay down certain conditions under which all bodies corporate desirous of establishing place of business in India must necessarily subject themselves to the discipline of law of this country by following the normal procedure of registration and incorporation under the law of the land. We are aware of the fact that advantage has been taken and is likely to be taken in future by persons incorporating themselves as a company under the very liberal laws obtaining in some countries and by operating their business from this country as foreign companies. This practice is

---

41. "Report of the High Powered Expert Committee on Companies and MRTP Acts," Ministry of Law, Justice and Company Affairs, Government of India, August 1977, pp. 26-27.

particularly objectionable when the real persons in the control of these companies happen to be Indian citizens." Following suggestions were given to rationalise the Companies Act *vis-a-vis* the foreign companies :

(1) In section 11, a new sub-section, *viz.*, sub-section (3) should be added to read as follows :

"(*a*) No body corporate incorporated outside India shall be allowed to establish or operate any place of business in India for the purpose of engaging in agriculture including plantation, production, processing, manufacturing or mining activities or for the distribution of goods produced in India or for generation of electricity or power of any kind or in construction activities, unless it is registered as a company under this Act ;

(*b*) No body corporate incorporated outside India of which not less than fifty per cent of the paid up share capital (whether equity or preference or partly equity or partly preference) is held by one or more citizens of India or by one or more bodies corporate incorporated in India, whether singly or in aggregate, shall be allowed to establish or operate a place of business in India unless it is registered as a company under this Act."

(2) Sub-sections (3), (4) and (5) of Section 11 may be re-drafted as sections (4), (5) and (6) respectively.

(3) Sub-section (2) of Section 591 may be deleted.

(4) All existing foreign companies which fall within sub-section (3) of Section 11 must register themselves under the new Act within a period of six months from the commencement thereof.

(5) The existing provisions relating to foreign companies should be streamlined to remove the existing obscurities on the lines indicated above and should then be made applicable to the existing foreign companies which do not fall within any of the categories mentioned in sub-section (3) of Section 11. For example, the provisions contained in Sections 603 to 608 dealing with prospectus issued by foreign companies may be deleted and suitable provisions made in Section 600 including the prospectus

provisions contained in Part III of the Act. In future, foreign companies, should be exempted from registration as company under the Act only if they do not fall within those categories. However, it is recommended that the provisions of clauses (c), (e) and (f) of Section 433, should be made applicable to foreign companies and all the provisions relating to winding up of companies, following the applicability of those clauses of Section 433, shall apply to foreign companies.

FOREIGN EXCHANGE REGULATION ACT, 1973 (FERA)

The FERA also places certain restrictions on the MNCs. Of late, it has tightened its regulations relating to entry and operations of MNCs. The Act forbids foreign companies from doing any of the following without the prior permission of the RBI. This section states that a person resident outside India or a person who is not a citizen of India but is resident in India or a Company (other than a banking company) which is not incorporated under any law in force in India or in which the non-resident interest (as defined in Explanation III to Section 26) is more than 40 per cent or any branch of such company shall not, except with the general or special permission of the RBI.

Section 28 Provides

(a) act or accept appointment as agent in India or any person or company in the trading or commercial transactions of such persons or company, or

(b) act or accept appointment as technical or management adviser in India of any person or company, or

(c) permit any trade mark, which he or it is entitled to use, to be used by any person or company for any direct or indirect consideration.

Section 29 imposes restrictions on establishment of place of business in India. It provides that

(a) the carrying on in India of an activity of a trading, commercial or industrial nature ;

(*b*) the establishment of a branch office or other place of business in India for carrying on a trading commercial or industrial activity ;

(*c*) the acquisition of the whole or any part of any undertaking in India or a person or company carrying on any trade, commerce or industry or purchase of the share in India to any such company ;

by a non-resident, a person who is not a citizen of India (even if he is resident in India) non-resident company and a company in which the non-resident interest is more than 40 per cent.

Section 76 of the FERA envisages the factots to be taken into account, the Central Government or the RBI, as the case may be shall, while giving or granting any permission or license under the Act.

The manner of enforcement of the equity dilution provisions have been left to the RBI which can withhold remittances of profits and dividends unless its directives are complied with. This is hardly a satisfactory situation. With-holding does not amount to forefeiture. It only adds to the value of shares and ultimately the share values get strengthened in the capital market and the beneficiary are the foreign company and foreign shareholders.

Secondly, it could lead to discriminatory practices by allowing one company to retain the same capital by permitting enlargement of capital base by fresh issue or issue of bonus shares so as to make existing share capital conform to the percentage (as happened in case of Colgate-Palmolive India Ltd.). There is thus no disinvestment but only greater extension of business with more profits accruing on the foreign holding. With even a minimum 40 per cent, the management decisions are still with that single block, because of the wide dispersal of balance equity among a large section of public. Even when financial institutions, like LIC or UTI are equity holders but their influence on decision making will be minimal in view of the possibility of the foreign shareholders representative on the Board striking a bargain with other members of the Board.

At the same time the Industrial Development Regulation Act 1951 should also be amended suitably. While providing for different concessions to the enterprises established in notified backward regions should be opened only for domestic firms and not to the MNCs. In the same manner various tax concessions provided under the Income Tax Act, 1961 in terms of depreciation allowances, development rebates, tax free facility for certain period should be done away with in reference to the MNCs establishing their units in notified backward regions simply to get the benefits of various concessions.

It is because of these deficiencies that there is a case for evolving a separate Act for dealing with MNCs so that confusions and duplications can be avoided and one authority can control the activities of the MNCs.

SUMMARY AND CONCLUSIONS

Introduction

Objectives of the Study

Hypotheses and Methodology

Political Economy of Multinational Corporations

Cases of Political Involvement : Suggestions

Transfer of Technology

Case Studies—Conclusions and Suggestions

Transfer Pricing and Restrictive Business Practices

    (a) Transfer Pricing—Conclusions and Suggestions

    (b) Restrictive Business Practices

MNCs and Balance of Payments

Conclusions and Suggestions

Regulation of MNCs

National Entry Control System (NECS)

A Case for Separate Act

Suggestions

Summary and Conclusions

INTRODUCTION

Multinational Corporations are important actors on the world stage. The international production of these corporations including their affiliates and subsidiaries is somewhat larger than the total exports of all economies. The value added of all multinational corporations is roughly one-fifth of the world's gross national product excluding the centrally planned economies. Their annual sales are more than the gross national product of many developing countries.

The rise of multinational corporations has been one of the most remarkable phenomena of the post-war period. Of course, they had their existence as back as three to four hundred years ago. They are defined as firms which command production and distribution activities in more than one country. They are big and dynamic enterprises with operations in many product lines and in many countries growing at a spectacular rate. Their activities are globally co-ordinated by groups of persons, organised in their head offices, exercising tight control on men, money and markets. They derive strength from their vast capital, sophisticated technology and trade names. If their growth continues at the same rate it did during the period 1970-75 and 1975-80 by the end of this century their share will rise to nearly half of the total product of the world economy, excluding the centrally planned economies. Indeed the whole capitalist economy may very well be dominated by some 200 giant corporations of which three-fourths may be American based.

In this Chapter a summary of this study and its conclusions are given. The whole study has been divided into seven chapters (including the present one) dealing with different facets of developmental implications of the operations of the multinational corporations in developing countries especially in reference to the Indian economy. Though the conclusions and suggestions have been given in the respective chapters but here they are all presented in the shape of a summary.

OBJECTIVES OF THE STUDY

Chapter I deals with brief historical background, origin of multinational corporations and with the conceptual framework. It deals with the analysis of the power of multinational corporations on account of their sales and world wide network. 50 top ranking (as per the FURTUNE list) multinationals are discussed in this connection (200 top ranking multinationals have been shown in the Appendix II). How the flow of funds (investment, profit, etc.) from the host economies to parent firms' countries have adversely affected the development of the third world countries in variety of ways have been analysed in this chapter. At the same time the investment pattern of multinational corporations in the Indian economy has been discussed at length with the help of analysing their size and rate of growth in their assets and investments in different sectors of the Indian economy. This chapter also deals with the objectives and methodology of the study. In brief the objectives of the study are three fold—

(*a*) the objective of asserting developing countries', especially India's sovereignty over their own political and economic life ;

(*b*) the objective of compelling or persuading the foreign corporations to make more contribution to developing countries' growth and welfare or to fall in line with the national priorities ; and

(*c*) the objective of emancipating the under-developed countries from having to contribute 'captive production' to a vertically integrated corporate system that did not subserve host countries' interest.

HYPOTHESES AND METHODOLOGY

The following hypotheses were formulated for this study—

(*a*) that the multinational corporations are responsible for disturbing the resource base and solely function to their advantage against the interest of the host countries ;

(*b*) that the multinational corporations are interfering, and at times conflicting, with the local administration and thus eroded the sovereignty of the nation States ;

(*c*) that the transfer of technology is nothing but farce and the host countries are being flushed with the inappropriate technology not suited to their conditions ;

(*d*) that the development of the international trade and the impact on the balance of payment thereof is going against the third world in general and India in particular due to the operation of multinational corporations. Common practices adopted by the multinational corporations are, *inter alia*, transfer pricing, inter-corporate investments, restrictive business practices, etc. ;

(*e*) that the capitalistic methods of production employed by the MNCs to produce for the 'class' and not for the 'mass' are giving rise to the exploitation of consumers in particular and society at large.

The methodology deals with the type of the data utilised and method employed for them. Generally the published secondary source of data have been utilised on account of their authenticity. Though the questionnaire was prepared and sent to some of the concerns related to the multinational corporations but the response was very poor as it happens in such studies. Non-availability of data was one of the most formidable problems. Sample data were taken separately for individual chapters dealing with different developmental problems relating to the multinational corporations' activities.

POLITICAL ECONOMY OF THE MNCs

Chapter II deals with the Political Economy of Multinational Corporations. On the basis of enormous financial and political power of the MNCs it was concluded that these corporations have become the instruments of foreign policy of the parent firms' countries. With their international network they used to align with separatist forces supporting to some and sabotaging the others have come as an important threat to the national sovereignty. Examples of toppling the governments by the multinational corporations are also there.

CASES OF POLITICAL INVOLVEMENT

Various proved cases of the MNCs' involvement in such political wranglings have been quoted in case of South Africa, Rhodesia, Mozambique, Chile, Katanga, Sumatra, Indonesia, Brazil, Argentina, Peru, Nicaragua, Sri Lanka, Honduras, Jamaica and India. The ITT case of Chile has been separately dealt with in detail. Many such examples are given in Indian situation where the MNCs flouted the government decisions by political interference and compelled the local administration to change the policy and putting the State exchequer at loss.

SUGGESTIONS

Following suggestions are advanced for this state of affairs :

1. There may be a complete restriction on the entrance of the multinational corporations. Hundred per cent indigenous firms and technology should be preferred. Though this may give an extremistic view of the situation but countries will have to do it as China did in its early stages of development. Multinational corporations should be allowed only when a country's economy is in self-sustaining stage of growth. The fact is that even the developed countries of today restricted such foreign investments in their countries to protect their economies. For example, the Australian government's committee of Economic Enquiry recommended to the Parliament in September 1965 to limit the 'new overseas investment' to an annual level of 336 million dollars. The French government's policy of curtailing new foreign affiliates in 1963 was directed largely against the potential dominance of particular industry sectors. Japan not only restricted the aggregate inflow of foreign equity but also effectively kept foreign investors out of 'strategic' and 'key' industries such as

electricals, chemicals and automobiles. Such restrictions would be effective in reducing tensions arising from the spread of multi-national enterprises.

2. If the foreign collaboration is at all necessary the firms from and to the developing countries should be encouraged. Because most of the developing countries have nearly identical problems or developmental priorities. This will not only boost the development potentials of the less developed countries but also expand and develop the markets and additional generation of wealth and income will help these countries instead of concentrating in the hands of few capitalist countries of the world. The developing countries produce most of the world's raw material and primary goods and this is again a favourable aspect of forming the MNCs from developing countries. It should be very well understood that the interest of developed nations and developing nations are bound to clash and so with the multi-nationals.

3. There should be a legislation for preventing the multi-nationals from taking part in any type of political activity directly or indirectly. If some multinational firm is found to have involved in such activities it must be declared as *persona non grata* and even its business activities must be declared illegal unequivocally. There should be an independent body, with assertive rights, to keep constant watch on the foreign firms' activities related to its business or otherwise.

4. The governments of the less developed countries could use one important bargaining advantage they possess—control over the access to their territory. But the less developed countries being the soft State this seems to be very difficult. One of the major problems is that MNCs too have control over certain resources required for the development of these countries. The less developed countries' desire for pseudo benefit of foreign direct investment poses an important dilemma for the policy makers. On the one hand they do not want to make regulations so restrictive that it will deter potential investor and another factor weakening the bargaining power of LDCs is the absence of competition for investment opportunities. Furthermore, it is said and felt by the interested groups, sometimes explicitly,

that even if a country resolves the dilemma in favour of regulation, their remain important constraints on the ability of the country to carry out regulatory policies. But this is the time when the economic administrators will have to choose between the two. There should not be any compromising via-media for such an enormous problem threatening the very sovereignty of the nations.

TRANSFER OF TECHNOLOGY

Chapter III attempts to discuss the question of transfer of technology from MNCs to the developing countries. This deals with the strategy for transfer of technology adopted by the MNCs and their impact on production, export and imports and overall performance of such technology transfer. Also various restrictions placed by the MNCs for diffusing the technology are also considered. The issues related to the transfer of technology discussed is this chapter are :

(*a*) license and patents

(*b*) research and development activities in LDCs

(*c*) adaptability of products and processes to local conditions, and

(*d*) linkage to the host country's domestic economy.

CASE STUDIES

A case study of Indian Engineering Industry has been cited on account of the fact that this industry is a high technology oriented industry. A sample of 60 units was taken and divided into four clusters according to the degree of foreign association. It was concluded that higher the degree of foreign association higher was the import intensity and lower was the export potentiality (export performance index). In fact, in the name of the sophisticated technology the developing countries were provided with the obsolete and inappropriate technology. On the other hand, lower degree of foreign association units fared well in their export performance and helped in reducing the imports.

Then a separate discussion is devoted to the case study of Gabriel (India) Limited which has received technology from Gabriel Company, USA. The payment made by the Indian counterpart to the US company is much more than what it has received. At the same time the foreign company has protected its overseas market in the USA, France, Italy, Spain, Argentina, Mexico and Japan by prohibiting the Indian counterpart to export to these markets. Attempt has been made to spell out the structure of technology in the developing countries ; basic characteristics of technology transfer ; the form of technology transfer ; restrictive practices attached with the technology transfer ; and cost of technology to the less developed countries.

A brief reference has also been made of Indian Dyestuff industry which has confirmed the above conclusions. Then recent technical collaborations with foreign companies were also discussed about the Graphite Vicarb India Limited (collaborating with French Vicarb SA), Lorcom (Protectives) Ltd. with LRC Overseas Ltd., UK.

Cases have been cited for the impact on employment and human resources development also.

CONCLUSIONS AND SUGGESTIONS

It was concluded that the technology is the key to economic power in the modern world. Global corporations, as we have seen, are for the most part oligopolies. Their enviable position usually rests on some piece of exclusive technology which they are not anxious to make available to actual or potential competitors. At the same time if they are to operate globally they are forced to spread their technology. But the poor countries are likely to get processes which are abandoned elsewhere or on the verge of abandonment. Distributing the last generation's technology to the developing countries is a good way to prolong its profitable life. Thus in many cases the imported technology is too expensive and too complicated. Having been developed for the needs of industrialised societies, it does not solve and rather aggravate the problem in developing countries.

There is no doubt that the imported technology has had a

major impact on developing countries, but not the positive effects as hoped and claimed. Of course, there are certain studies which have been devoted to their positive effects but again the imperialistic bias of such studies could not be ruled out. There is no doubt that the interests of technology suppliers and the recipients do often clash in one way or the other. It is plausible that the assumed efficiency of the manufacturing units closely associated with the multinational corporations may be the result of their operations in an oligopolistic/monopolistic structure that prevail in the protected markets. It is in this context that one has to interpret the oft-repeated argument that foreign collaboration in the process of import substitution may lead to negative trade impact but does not prelude great possibility of income generation. In a sense, therefore, it is the institutional structure in the developing countries that makes the multinationals appear most efficient rather than its built-in characteristics. To get rid of this situation following suggestions can be given.

1. There should be an independent national agency to screen and review the technology which is proposed to be transferred from the multinationals. This body should be named by the technocrats. Every technology transfer proposal must be approved by this agency. This will help in making the appropriate technology available to the host countries.

2. The firm selling/transferring technology to the developing countries should be asked, on a mandatory basis, to establish the R and D facilities in the host countries. This will provide for host country's participation in the R and D activities which hitherto is not there.

3. All the technical collaboration agreements must be viewed keeping in mind the various restrictive clauses, over pricing (at the international standard) and the clauses making a recurring liability (like payment of royalty, etc.) on the domestic firms and on the foreign exchange resources of the recipient country.

4. At the same time all academic institutions and the researches going on in these institutions must have vocational relationship with the industry and trade. This will

give better opportunities to domestic potential of the scientific personnel and commercial uses thereof. Most of the technical researches are still to reach the stage of industrial application in developing countries in general and India in particular. This will not only help in checking the 'brain drain' but will also boost the development in the country itself.

TRANSFER PRICING AND RESTRICTIVE BUSINESS PRACTICES

(a) Transfer Pricing

Chapter IV attempts to highlight the problems of transfer pricing and restrictive business practices, the motives behind adopting such practices and their developmental implications. In this section the transfer pricing for our analysis was defined as—

$$Pc - Pw/Pw \times 100$$

Where Pc Price actually paid in a country under study

Where Pw comparable world market price. It was found that the underlying considerations for adopting the practice of transfer pricing were mainly—maximisation of profits, minimisation of risks and uncertainty arising from balance of payments needs, political and social pressures etc. Effects and extent of transfer pricing have been dealt with at length with the citation of cases in support of such practices in India and elsewhere. At the same time various difficulties faced in analysing the transfer pricing practices are also discussed which are mainly—the uneven incidence of transfer pricing across different industries and by the different firms ; problems in collecting the data relating to the transfer pricing ; and conceptual issues in defining correct transfer prices.

CONCLUSIONS AND SUGGESTIONS

Regarding the transfer pricing the conclusions drawn are—

(a) that the trade on the basis of transfer pricing today accounts for a substantial part of the world trade, and will account for a larger proportion in the future if the multinational corporations continue to grow.

(*b*) that the declared earnings of the MNCs are very much smaller than the value of intra-firm trade, so that a relatively mino change in transfer prices can cause a very large change in MNCs' profitability.

(*c*) that the available evidence indicates that transfer pricing is deliberately used to transfer profits from less desirable to more desirable areas, and the existing inbuilt constraints to its use are ineffective.

It may be suggested here that the transfer pricing mechanism of the MNCs is highly complex and thus difficult to check. But as a matter of an honest effort the following suggestions can be ventured—

1. The government should try to break the link between imports and parent companies by channelling all imports through an independent State agency of forcing firms to buy elsewhere. But this require a large administrative commitment.

2. The tax authority should try to judge profits of the MNCs on evidences other than declared profits, say, their profitability abroad, or their sales, or some other such measures. But this may become extremely arbitrary, contentious. Yet it has got to be done.

3. The government may decide to check transfer prices directly and compare them with the world prices. This may seem difficult but the international indices may be used for this purpose. The dispute may arise only in case of items when they are not openly traded on the world markets. Here the use of consultants may be of great help.

4. All the host governments may get together and tax them jointly, rendering the whole process of profit transfer irrelevant. This may be the most ideal solution.

5. The government may encourage internal checks to the use of transfer pricing by enlarging the share of local equity in the multinational corporations.

6. There should be direct official checks and its effectiveness can be increased by inter-government co-operation and exchange of information (as in the Andean Pact countries).

(*b*) **Restrictive Business Practices**

Restrictive business practices adopted by the multinational corporations have also been taken as one of the important dimensions of MNCs operations. Such practices were broadly classified in three main headings namely :

(*i*) aspect of pricing policies

(*ii*) territorial market and product allocation arrangement

(*iii*) forms of boycott and enforcement measures

Of course, various other types of restrictive business practices are also discussed at length. The implications of restrictive trade practices are considered in terms of the following :

(*i*) Natural resource development

(*ii*) Output

(*iii*) Employment

(*iv*) Income distribution

(*v*) Resource allocation

Regarding the restrictive trade practices it was concluded that the whole world can be divided into two so far as the restrictive business practices are concerned. One, the RBP intensive sector, represented by developing countries and second, non-RBP sector represented by developed countries. However, the latter countries too have RBPs but incidence of such practices are higher in case of the 'former. It goes without saying that the RBPs used by the multinational corporations prove to be a great threat to the host countries' economies and they must be checked before they go against the economic development requirement of these countries. Various types of RBPs used by the MNCs in one way or the other, should be effectively checked either through legislative action or administrative acumen. Many RBPs have diverted the meagre economic resources of the countries to non-developmental channels. Moreover, the multinational corporations are reaping advantages from the use of natural resources of the host countries which could have been otherwise used for these countries.

MNCs AND BALANCE OF PAYMENTS

In Chapter 5 the implications of MNC's operations on the host countries' balance of payment are discussed. This includes the overall impact of investment and trade flows by the MNCs on the balance of payment of host developing countries. Also it includes the impact of other outflows in terms of payment for technology transfer ; remittances in the form of dividends, royalties, commission etc. ; transfer pricing and others on balance of payments. On the basis of a study of 159 samples (11 in Jamaica, 8 in Kenya, 53 in India, 15 in Malaysia, 16 in Iran, and 56 in Columbia) it was concluded that in 145 cases (8 in Jamaica, 3 in Kenya, 48 in India, 14 in Malaysia, 16 in Iran and 56 in Columbia) the balance of payments effect was negative. On the basis of a pedagogic Table (Table 5.3) it was inferred that in the long run the foreign investment are the real burden on host country's economy. conclusions of the greater outflow, as compared to inflow, were drawn by the RBI also in the Indian case. The analysis is made upto 1977-78 because of non-availability of authentic information after that period. Here the authenticity of information was Considered of prime importance. Of course, the recent data have been incorporated in some cases like Colgate Palmolive India Ltd., Ashok Leyland, ITD Ltd., Parke-Davis, May and Baker, Guest Keen Williams and Firestone Rubber (now the Modistone).

CONCLUSIONS AND SUGGESTIONS

What is concluded is that the impact of MNCs on Indian balance of payment in general have been negative. Various outflows on account of dividend remittances, royalties, technical fees and payment to foreign technicians, import of raw materials and spares in foreign currency have far exceeded the inflow on account of investment in cash and kind, exports, etc. On the other hand the Indian companies have fared better not only in terms of balance of payments but also in terms of their export performance and import intensity.

Lack of data on intra-firm trading, under the counter remittances in one way or the other have in, no doubt, exercised a drain on already meagre resources of the host developing countries. At the same time the developing nations are deprived of the benefits of international trade by their being oligopolistic in structure, their vertical and horizontal integration, their interlocking directorates and their cross-subsidisation of activities together with their massive access to financial resources. The dream of operation of new world economic order could perhaps not become true unless a serious thought is given to the significance and remification of the multinational corporations in context of global economic system. By sheer idea of transferring their investment/assets from one country to another could place the host country's economy in jeopardy, especially of those which are small countries like that of Africa's and Latin America's.

It is, therefore, suggested that ;

1. The developing countries should consider including provisions in their initial agreement with the multinational corporations which permit the possibility of reduction over time of the percentage of foreign ownership ; the term as far as possible should be agreed upon at the very beginnning.

2. Before entering into any agreement the balance of payment implications of an MNC's activities must be given a serious thought. In case it appears to cause any negative impact on the balance of payments such foreign investments or technology should be discouraged, unless and otherwise required for serving the national interest.

3. Where ownership is an important objective for the host countries, consideration should be given to the establishment of joint ventures as well as to the reduction over time of the share of foreign equity interests.

4. The host countries should explore alternative ways of importing technology other than by foreign direct investment, and should acquire the capacity to determine which technology would best suit their needs. Help may be solicited from international institutions if need be.

5. The home and host countries both should enforce arm's length pricing whenever appropriate ; and should elaborate rules

on pricing practices for tax purposes. This will help doing away with the overinvoicing and under-invoicing problems and their probable impact on the balance of payments position.

REGULATION OF MNCs

Chapter 6 deals with the regulation of the multinational corporations. It discusses the choice between national regulatory system and international regulatory system. It is attempted to submit that preference should be given to the national regulatory system of course, with keeping in mind the existence of international conventions and codes. But in case of deciding any matter relating to the MNCs the former should prevail and the national interest must be the commanding consideration. A detailed analysis has been made for the existing regulatory system and various efforts made at the international and regional level to control and regulate the activities of multinational corporations. It is generally seen that no country has separate acts to deal with the activities of the multinational corporations exclusively but they are having fragmented pieces of legislation to regulate the domestic and foreign industrial enterprises alike. Somewhere more provisions have been inserted in the existing regulatory system regarding the control of foreign direct investment. But this has resulted in duplication and lot of confusion among the executors of such regulations. Also the multinational corporations do take the advantage out of the multiplicity of regulations.

Existing Regulatory System in India

In India there are so many acts applied to domestic and foreign enterprises alike. These are, Companies Act, 1956 ; Foreign Exchange Regulation Act, 1973 ; Foreign Money Contribution Act, Industrial Development and Regulation Act, 1951 ; Monopolies and Restrictive Trade Practices Act, 1969 and host of others. Arguments for controlling the activities of the multinational corporations are briefly given in this chapter so as to enable us to see the regulatory system in that light. Three points are given due thought before formulating the control mechanism, namely, nature of control ; entities to be covered ;

and means for effective control. Then ten directive principles have been spelled out to consider before embarking on some regulatory system.

NATIONAL ENTRY CONTROL SYSTEM (NECS)

A National Entry Control System to mean a collection of certain regulations directed at both entry and operational phases of foreign direct investment projects is considered to be an effective medium of control. The NEC System was studied in many countries like, Columbia, Brazil, Argentina, Mexico, Venezuela, India Indonesia, Malaysia, Philippines, Thailand, Portugal, Algeria and Kenya. It was found that there were eight common elements in all these countries as part of the control system. These were :

Sectors—the sectors where the foreign direct investment was to be directed ;

Geography—planning greater amounts of foreign direct investment in desired geographical location of the host country ;

Ownership—emphasising on more local ownership as proportion to the total ownership pattern ;

Acquisition—regulating the number of local firms being acquired by the multinational corporations ;

Content—requiring a given level of local contents in foreign direct investment based production ;

Export—requiring a given level of exports of multinationals' output ;

Employment—regulating the number of foreign employees at various levels of employment of such projects ;

Repatriation—restricting repatriation of profits and capital.

The chapter also deals with the implications of the NECS while discussing the relationship between the less developed countries and the multinational corporations. In this connection three widely held opinions—the Sovereignty at Bay Model, the Dependencia Model and the Mercantilist Model—were discussed.

The possible impacts of NECS on various characteristics of foreign direct investment and technical collaboration are also discussed.

A CASE FOR SEPARATE ACT

Still there is a case for separate legislation to deal with the activities of the multinational corporations. In India also there is a multiplicity of such legislations. This state of affairs do not help in achieving the ends of controlling them in the national interest. Thus there is a case for a separate enactment to deal with the activities of the multinational corporations. Until such enactment is there the existing Companies Act, 1956 and Foreign Exchange Regulation Act, 1973 should be suitably amended.

Companies Act, 1956

It may be suggested that the present position regarding the foreign companies is quite unsatisfactory. The practice of first allowing certain bodies corporate incorporated outside India to be registered as foreign companies and then apply a large number of sections in the Act, not otherwise applicable to them by making indirect provisions here and there and from time to time, is wrong. Instead, it would be desirable to lay down certain conditions under which all bodies corporate desirous of establishing place of business in India must necessarily subject themselves to the discipline of law of this country by following the normal procedure of registration and incorporation under the law of the land. We are aware of the fact that advantage has been taken and is likely to be taken in future by persons incorporating themselves as a company under the very liberal laws obtaining in some countries and operating their business from this country as foreign companies. This practice is particularly objectionable when the real persons controlling these companies happen to be the Indian citizens.

SUGGESTIONS

Following suggestions are given to rationalise the Companies Act *vis-a-vis* the foreign companies :

1. In section 11, a new sub-section, *viz.*, sub-section (3) should be added to read as follows :

"(*a*) No body corporate incorporated outside India shall be allowed to establish or operate any place of business in India for the purpose of engaging in agriculture including plantation, production, processing, manufacturing or mining activities or for the distribution of goods produced in India or for generation of electricity or power of any kind or in construction activities, unless it is registered as a company under this Act ;

(*b*) No body corporate incorporated outside India of which not less than fifty per cent of the paid-up share capital (whether equity or preference or partly equity or partly preference) is held by one or more citizens of India or by one or bodies corporate incorporated in India, whether singly or in aggregate shall be allowed to establish or operate a place of business in India unless it is registered as a company under this Act."

2. Sub-sections (3), (4) and (5) of Section 11 may be redrafted as Sections (4), (5) and (6) respectively.

3. Sub-section (2) of Section 591 may be deleted.

4. All existing foreign companies which fall within sub-section (3) of Section 11 must register themselves under the new Act within a period of six months from the commencement thereof.

5. The existing provisions relating to foreign companies should be streamlined to remove the existing obscurities on the lines indicated above and should then be made applicable to the existing foreign companies which do not fall within any of the categories mentiond in sub-section (3) of Section 11. For example, the provisions contained in Sections 603 and 608 dealing with prospectus issued by foreign companies may be deleted and suitable provisions made in Section 600 including the prospectus provisions contained in Part III of the Act. In future, the foreign companies, should be exempted from registration as company under the Act only if they do not fall in those categories. However, it is recommended that the provisions of clauses (c), (e) and

(f) of Section 433, should be made applicable to foreign companies and all the provisions relating to winding up of companies, following the applicability of those clauses of Section 433, shall apply to foreign companies.

Foreign Exchange Regulation Act and IDR

The position regarding the FERA is also not satisfactory so far as the multinational corporations are concerned. Sections 26 and 28 are not very much clear as to what exactly it seeks to do. The manner of enforcement of the equity dilution provisions have been left to the RBI which can withhold remittances of profits and dividends unless its directives are complied with. This is hardly a satisfactory situation. Withholding does not amount to forefeiture. It only adds to the value of shares and ultimately the share values get strengthened in the capital market and the beneficiary are the foreign companies and foreign shareholders.

Secondly, it could lead to discriminatory practices by allowing one company to retain the same capital by permitting enlargement of capital base by fresh issue or issue of bonus shares so as to make existing share capital conform to the percentage (as happened in the case of Colgate Palmolive India Ltd.). There is thus no disinvestment but only greater extension of business with more profits accruing on the foreign holding. With even a minimum forty per cent, the management decisions are still with that single block, because of the wide dispersal of balance equity among a large section of the public. Even when the financial institutions like LIC, UTI are equity holders but their influence on the decision-making will remain minimal in view of the possibility of the foreign shareholders representative on the Board striking a bargain with other members of the Board.

At the same time the Industrial Development and Regulation Act, 1951 should be amended suitably. The scheduling pattern of establishing the industrial units must be revamped particularly in the light of the foreign enterprises. The list of items reserved for indigenous firms and small scale sector should be strictly complied with. Similarly, the host of fiscal concessions provided under the Income Tax Act, 1961 should also be withdrawn in case of the multinational corporations. The concessions relating to the industrially backward areas should not be made available to the multinationals but only to the domestic concerns. It has been seen that in the name of the various concessions the multinational firms have remitted abroad many a times of funds what they invested and without paying any tax to the Indian government.

But the ultimate remedy lies in the separate Act for the multinationals and change in the attitude towards the 'phoren' euphoria

Appendices

The International 200 (Outside U.S.)

Rank 83'	Company	Country	Industry	Sales $000
1.	Royal Dutch/ Shell Group	Neth./ Britain	Petroleum	80,550,885
2.	British Petroleum	Britain	Petroleum	49,194,886
3.	ENI	Italy	Petroleum	25,002,358
4.	IRI	Italy	Metal mfg.- Steel, shipbldg.; aerospace	24,518,447
5.	Unilever	Britain/ Neth.	Food products ; Soops, cosmetics	20,291,583
6.	Toyota Motor	Japan	Motor vehicles	19,741,094
7.	Francaise des Petroles	France	Petroleum	18,350,186
8.	Elf-Aquitaine	France	Petroleum	18,188,156
9.	Matsushita Electric Industrial	Japan	Electronics, appliances	16,719,440
10.	Petrobras (petroleo Brasileiro)	Brazil	Petroleum	16,258,011
11.	Philips Gloeilampenfabrieken	Netherland	Electronics, appliances	16,176,941
12.	Pemex (Petroleos Mexicanos)	Mexico	Petroleum	16,140,013
13.	Hitachi	Japan	Electronics, appliances, office equipment	15,804,301
14.	Siemens	Germany	Electronics ; computers	15,724,273
15.	Nissan Motor	Japan	Motor vehicles	15,697,733

187

1	2	3	4	5
16. Volkswagenwerk	Germany	Motor vehicles	15,693,352
17. Daimler-Benz	Germany	Motor vehicles and parts	15,660,437
18. Bayer	Germany	Chemicals	14,615,594
19. Hoechst	Germany	Chemicals	14,558,235
20. Renault	France	Motor vehicles and parts	14,467,765
21. Fiat	Italy	Motor vehicles and parts	14,466,548
22. Nestle	Switzerland	Food products ; beverages	13,303,618
23. BASF	Germany	Chemicals	13,250,424
24. Volvo	Sweden	Motor vehicles and parts ; energy	12,963,008
25. Imperial Chemical Industries	Britain	Chemicals	12,750,075
26. BAT Industries	Britain	Tobacco	12,083,087
27. Mitsubishi Heavy Industries	Japan	Motor vehicles ; industrial equipment	11,916,259
28. Nippon Steel	Japan	Metal Manufacturing-steel	11,605,901
29. Thyssen	Germany	Metal mfg.-steel industrial equip.	11,301,248
30. Peugeot	France	Motor vehicles and parts	11,244,484
31. General Motors of Canada	Canada	Motor vehicles and parts	11,200,522
32. Idemitsu Kosan	Japan	Petroleum	10,770,203
33. Kuwait Petroleum	Kuwait	Petroleum	10,744,273
34. Canadian Pacific	Canada	Metal manufacturing-steel, mining	10,351,766
35. Toshiba	Japan	Electronics, appliances	9,482,937
36. Esso UK	Britain	Petroleum	9,448,316
37. Hyundai Group	South Korea	Shipbuilding, motor vehicles,	

1	2	3	4	5
			industrial equip.	9,300,429
38.	Indian Oil	India	Petroleum	9,069,891
39.	Honda Motor	Japan	Motor vehicles and parts	8,771,902
40.	Petrofina	Belgium	Petroleum	8,717,574
41.	National Coal Board	Britain	Mining-coal	8,242,117
42.	CGE (cie, General d' Electricite)	France	Electronics, appliances	8,195,173
43.	General Electric Co.	Britain	Electronics ; industrial equip.	7,730,745
44.	Saint-Gobain	France	Building materials; metal products	7,595,596
45.	Veba Oel	Germany	Petroleum, chemicals	7,570,949
46.	Rio Tinto-Zinc	Britain	Mining-alum, lead, zinc, copper, iron	7,292,903
47.	Imperial Oil	Canada	Petroleum	7,236,088
48.	Ruhrkohle	Germany	Mining-coal	7,195,761
49.	Samsung Group	S. Korea	Electronics, appliances, food produ.; textiles	7,167,315
50.	Lucky Group	S. Korea	Petroleum, electronics, appliances	7,159,333
51.	Ciba-Geigy	Switzerland	Chemicals, pharmaceuticals	7,018,167
52.	Montedison	Italy	Chemicals	7,014,483
53.	Ford Motor of Canada	Canada	Motor vehicles and parts	6,961,541
54.	DSM	Netherlands	Natural gas ; chemicals	6,926,030
55.	YPF(Yacinientos Petroliferos)	Argentina	Petroleum	6,782,765
56.	Fried, Krupp	Germany	Metal mfg.- steel ; industrial equipment	6,671,591

1	2	3	4	5
57.	Barlow Rand	S. Africa	Food products ; mining-coal, chrome, gold	6,747,692
58.	Maruzen Oil	Japan	Petroleum	6,638,171
59.	VOFST-Alpine	Austria	Metal manufacturing	6,632,500
60.	Thomson	France	Electronics, appliances	6,492,743
61.	Esso	Germany	Petroleum	6,397,340
62.	Daewoo Industrial	S. Korea	Shipbldg., textiles, elec. appl.; indus. equip.	6,313,466
63.	Nippon Kokan	Japan	Metal mfg.-steel	6,267,271
64.	Sankyong	S. Korea	Petroleum ; textiles ; chemical	6,210,191
65.	Mitshubishi Electric	Japan	Electronics. appl.	6,127,766
66.	Toyo Kogyo	Japan	Motor vehicles	6,050,038
67.	Grand Metropolitan	Britain	Beverages ; food products	6,044,617
68.	Petroleos de Venezuela	Venezuela	Petroleum	6,012,156
69.	Adam Opel	Germany	Motor vehicles and parts	5,871,961
70.	NEC	Japan	Electronics, appliances	5,783,079
71.	Rhone-Poulenc	France	Chemicals	5,656,879
72.	George Weston Holdings	Britain	Food products	5,642,132
73.	Robert Bosch	Germany	Motor vehicle parts ; electronics appliances	5,618,211
74.	Nippon Mining	Japan	Petroleum ; metal manufacturing-nonferrous	5,612,031
75.	Schlumberger	Neth. Antilles	Measuring and scientific equip.	5,513,246

1	2	3	4	5
76. Mannesmann	Germany	Metal products ; industrial equip.	5,509,361
77. Sumitomo Metal Industries	Japan	Metal manufacturing-steel	5,492,402
78. Ford Motor	Britain	Motor vehicles	5,434.433
79. British Steel	Britain	Metal manufacturing-steel	5,399,489
80. Michelin	France	Rubber products	5,390,093
81. Chinese Petroleum	Taiwan	Petroleum	5,313,672
82. Akzo Group	Netherlands	Chemicals	5,283,786
83. Toa Nenryo Kogyo	Japan	Petroleum	5,259,645
84. Ford-worke	Germany	Motor vehicles and parts	5,227,533
85. BL	Britain	Motor vehicles	5,185,374
86. Brown Boveri	Switzerland	Electrical and industrial equip. electronics	5,074,257
87. Daikyo Oil	Japan	Petroleum	5,004,090
88. Gutehoffnungshutte	Germany	Industrial and transportation equipment	4,988,056
89. Mitsubishi Oil	Japan	Petroleum	4,916,879
90. Kobe Steel	Japan	Metal manufacturing-steel	4,885,412
91. Sanyo Electric	Japan	Electronics, appliances	4,774,860
92. BMW (Bayerische Motoren Worko)	Germany	Motor vehicles and parts	4,675,261
93. Texaco Canada	Canada	Petroleum	4,645,570
94. Dalgety	Britain	Food products	4,587,804
95. Kawasaki Steel	Japan	Metal manufacturing-steel	4,581,474
96. Sony	Japan	Electronics, appl.	4,544,500
97. Thorn EMI	Britain	Electronics, appliances	4,538,679
98. AEG-Telefunken	Germany	Electronics, appliances	4,512,314
99. Degussa	Germany	Metal products ; chemicals	4,420,680

1	2	3	4	5
100. ENPETROL	Spain	Petroleum ; chemicals	4,399,869
101. Taiyo Fishery	Japan	Food products	4,295,935
102. Broken Hill Proprietary	Australia	Metal manu-facturing steel	4,288,760
103. Sacilor	France	Metal manu-facturing-steel	4,285,825
104. Mitsubishi Chemical Indus.	Japan	Chemicals	4,283,144
105. Neste	Finland	Petroleum	4,264,702
106. Usinor	France	Metal manu-facturing-steel	4,262,710
107. Alcan Aluminium	Canada	Metal manufac-turing-aluminium	4,225,311
108. Electrolux	Sweden	Electronics, appliances	4,189,713
109. Gulf Canada	Canada	Petroleum	4,119,840
110. IBM Deutschland	Germany	Office equipment (includes com-puters)	4,119,322
111. Norsk Hydro	Norway	Chemicals ; petroleum	4,077,339
112. ASEA	Sweden	Electronics, appliances, indus. equipment	3,939,863
113. Metallgesellschaft	Germany	Metal manufactu-ring-nonferrous	3,900,415
114. Flick Group	Germany	Paper and wood products ; chemi-cals	3,894,780
115. Solvay	Belgium	Chemicals, plastics	3,886,019
116. Showa Oil	Japan	Petroleum	3,868,399
117. Imperial Group	Britain	Tobacco ; food ; beverages	3,849,698
118. Turkiye Petrolleri	Turkey	Petroleum	3,837,624

1	2	3	4	5
119. Fujitsu	Japan	Office equipment (includes computers) ; elect.	3,834,482
120. Pechiney	France	Metal manufacturing-aluminium, steel	3,805,972
121. Salzgitter	Germany	Metal manufacturing-steel ; ship-building	3,774,092
122. Ishikawajima-Harima Hvy. Ind.	Japan	Industrial equip. shipbuilding	3,738,225
123. Pirelli	Switzerland	Rubber products	3,730,231
124. Allied-Lyons	Britain	Beverages ; food products	3,693,594
125. Mobil Oil	Germany	Petroleum	3,692,389
126. IBM France	France	Office equipment (includes computers)	3,673,509
127. Statoil	Norway	Petroleum	3,602,889
128. Roche/Sapac	Switzerland	Pharmaceuticals ; chemicals	3,575,547
129. Esso Italiana	Italy	Petroleum	3,534,970
130. Asahi Chemical Industry	Japan	Chemicals, textiles	3,502,996
131. Esso	France	Petroleum	3,497,013
132. Chrysler Canada	Canada	Motor vehicles and parts	3,487,345
133. British Aerospace	Britain	Aerospace	3,486,981
134. ALUSUISSE (Swiss Aluminium)	Switzerland	Metal manufacturing-aluminium	3,438,383
135. Sharp	Japan	Electronics ; appliances	3,438,090
136. L.M. Ericsson Telephone	Sweden	Electronics-telecommunications	3,359,499
37. Esso	Belgium	Petroleum ; chemicals	3,327,427

1	2	3	4	5
138.	BSN	France	Food products ; beverages	3,265,395
139.	Ssangyong Cement Industrial	S. Korea	Petroleum, building materials	3,256,599
140.	Kawasaki Heavy Industries	Japan	Ind. equip. ; shipbldg. ; transport equip.	3,251,212
141.	Petro-Canada	Canada	Petroleum	3,210,252
142.	Bridgestone Tire	Japan	Rubber products	3,207,559
143.	Courtaulds	Britain	Textiles	3,184,378
144.	Komatsu	Japan	Industrial equip.	3,160,862
145.	Aerospatiale	France	Aerospace	3,152,012
146.	Ultramar	Britain	Petroleum	3,118,319
147.	Sandoz	Switzerland	Pharmaceuticals ; dyes	3,116,540
148.	Canada Development crops.	Canada	Chemicals	3,111,137
149.	Nova, an Alberta crop.	Canada	Petroleum, petro-chemicals	3,101,648
150.	Snow Brand Milk products	Japan	Food products	3,089,753
151.	Cockerill Sambre	Belgium	Metal manufacturing-steel	3,088,789
152.	Isuzu Motors	Japan	Motor vehicles and parts	3,088,142
153.	Sumitomo Chemicals	Japan	Chemicals	3,066,667
154.	CEPSA (Espanola de Petroleos)	Spain	Petroleum	3,063,729
155.	Reed-international	Britain	Publishing, printing, paper, pulp	3,023,112
156.	Texaco	Britain	Petroleum	3,005,603
157.	Guest Keen and Nettlefolds	Britain	Motor vehicle parts	2,993,107
158.	BTR	Britain	Industrial equip, build. materials	2,985,528
159.	Nippondenso	Japan	Motor vehicle parts	2,961,173

1	2	3	4	5
160.	Deutsche Texaco	Germany	Petroleum	2,938,815
161.	Koc Holding	Turkey	Motor vehicles and parts, metal production	2,928,141
162.	Steel Authority of India	India	Metal manufacturing-steel	2,926,635
163.	Koor Industries	Israel	Electronics ; fabricated metal prod. ; food	2,900,000
164.	Toray Industries	Japan	Chemicals	2,897,625
165.	BICC	Britain	Industrial equip.	2,882,599
166.	Beecham Group	Britain	Pharmaceuticals ; soops, cosmetics, beverages	2,844,967
167.	Deufsche Babcock	Germany	Metal products ; industrial equipment	2,822,181
168.	Asahi Glass	Japan	Building materials ; chemicals	2,784,277
169.	EFIM	Italy	Metal manufacturing ; aerospace ; metal prod.	2,780,130
170.	Unigate	Britain	Food products	2,777,620
171.	Conon	Japan	Photographic equip. office machines	2,768,328
172.	Saab-Scania	Sweden	Motor vehicles	2,707,397
173.	Northern Telecom	Canada	Telecommunications equipment	2,680,609
174.	BOC Group	Britain	Chemicals, gas, industrial equipment	2,655,561

1	2	3	4	5
175. OMV		Austria	Petroleum	2,625,680
176. Ranks Hovis Mcdougall		Britain	Food products	2,601,608
177. Saarbergwerke		Germany	Petroleum, mining coal	2,581,245
178. Cadbury Schweppes		Britain	Food products; beverages	2,581,242
179. IBM Japan		Japan	Office equipment (includes computers)	2,578,368
180. Fuji Photo Film		Japan	Chemicals	2,558,598
181. IBM United Kingdom Holdings		Britain	Office equipment (including computers)	2,542,132
182. Bertelsmann		Germany	Publishing, printing	2,517,082
183. Noranda Inc.		Canada	Metal manufacturing-non-ferrous, mining	2,515,066
184. Dai Nippon printing		Japan	Publishing, printing	2,507,263
185. Hiram Walker Resources		Canada	Beverages; Petroleum	2,478,919
186. Bowater		Britain	Paper and Wood products	2,459,820
187. CSR		Australia	Sugar; mining; building materials chemicals	2,459,274
188. Olivetti		Italy	Office equipment (includes computers	2,458,503
189. Conoco		Britain	Petroleum	2,453,453
190. Rothmans International		Britain	Tobacco	2,447,735
191. Oil and Natural Gas Commission		India	Petroleum	2,434,559
192. Koa Oil		Japan	Petroleum	2,433,796

1	2	3	4	5
193.	Dunlop Holdings	Britain	Rubber products	2,429,957
194.	Canada Packers	Canada	Food products	2,423,489
195.	Korea Explosives Group	S.Korea	Petroleum, chemicals	2,416,578
196.	Kubota	Japan	Industrial and farm equip. ; fab. met. prod.	2,413,325
197.	Philippine National Oil	Philippines	Petroleum	2,407,697
198.	Burmah Oil	Britain	Petroleum ; motor vehicle parts	2,393,425
199.	Lafarge Coppee	France	Building materials	2,373,118
200.	Rank Xerox	Britain	Office equipment	2,367,904

Distribution of 60 Sample Units of Selected Engineering Products in Various Clusters of Foreign Association

Product Groups	Cluster I	Cluster II	Cluster III	Cluster IV	Total
Cables and Wires	—	4	4	5	13
Textile Machinery	—	4	3	—	7
Transformers and Switchgears	2	5	3	4	14
Tyres and Tubes	3	3	2	—	8
Dry Cell and Storage Batteries	2	3	—	3	8
Electronic Products	3	3	2	2	10
TOTAL	10	22	14	14	60

Bibliography

1. ABRAHAM, Neville ; *Big Business and Government* : *The New Disorder*, Macmillan, 1974.

2. ANSHEN, Melvin and BACH, George L ; *Business Management in the 1980s*, McGraw Hill, New York, 1960.

3. AGRAWAL, H.P. ; *Business Collaboration in India*, Aruna Publications, New Delhi, 1982.

4. ASSOCIATION, American Accounting ; *Social and Political Impact of Multinationals on Third World Countries*, 60th Annual Meeting, August 23-25, 1976.

5. ARGENTI, John ; *Coporate Collapse* : *The Causes and Symptoms*, McGraw Hill, 1976.

6. AVERSKONG, K. ; *Foreign Direct Investment and Capital Formation in Developing Countries*, New York University Graduate School of Business Administration, Working Paper No. 73-10.

7. ARPAN. J.S. ; *International Inter-Corporate Pricing*, Praeger, New York, 1972.

8. BANNOCK, Graham ; *The Juggernauts* : *The Age of the Big Corporations*, Weidenfeld and Nicolson, 1971, Penguin, 1973.

9. BARNET, Richard J. and ¦MULLER, Ronald E. ; *Global Reach* : *The Power of Multinational Corporations*, Jonathan Cape, London, 1975.

10. BROWN, C.C. (ed.) ; *World Business*, Macmillan, 1970.

11. BEHRMAN. Jack N. ; *National Interest and Multinational Enterprises*, Englewood Cliffs, Prentice Hall, 1970.

12. BEHRMAN, Jack N. ; *Some Patterns in the rise of Multi-national Enterprises*, Chapel Hill, NC, Graduate School of Business Administration, University of North Carolina, 1969.

13. BARAN, Paul A, and SWEEZY, Paul M. ; *Monopoly Capital*, Monthly Review Press, 1966.

14. BELL, Daniel ; *The Coming of Post-industrial Society : A Venture in Social Forecasting*, Arnold Heinemann, London, 1974.

15. BROOKE, M.Z. and REMMERS, H.L. ; *The Strategy of Multinational Enterprises*, Longman, London, 1970.

16. BHAGWATI, J.N. ; *Economies of the World Order*, Orient Longman, Bombay, 1972.

17. BUCKLEY, Peter J. and CASSON, Mark ; *The Future of the Multinational Enterprise*, Macmillan, London, 1976.

18. BOARMAN, Patrick M. and SCHOLLHAMMER, Hans (ed.); *Multinational Corporations and Governments : Business Government Relations in an International Context*, Praeger, New York, 1975.

19. BALASUBRAMANYAM, V.N. ; *International Transfer of Technology in India*, Praeger, New York, 1973.

20. BARANSON, Jack ; *International Transfer of Automative Technology to Developing Countries*, New York, 1971.

21. —— *Technology and the Multinationals' Corporate Strategy in a Changing World Economy*, Lexington Books, D.C. Heath & Co., Lexington, Massachusetts, 1978.

22. BALL, George W. ; *Global Companies : The Political Economy of the Business*, Prentice Hall, 1975.

23. BETHEKE, Volker ; *Multinational Firm and Developing Countries*, HWWA, Institute of Economic Research, Hamburg, Verlag Waltarchivs, 1976.

24. BHATT. V.V. ; *Impact of Foreign Aid on Indian Economic Development*, Papers read at the Indian Economic Conference, Calcutta, 1966, Popular Prakashan, 1967.

25. BERGSTON, C. Fred *et al* ; *American Multinationals and American Interests*, Brooking Institution, Massachusetts.

26. CHEN, Edward K.Y.; *Multinational Corporations*, Technology and Employment, Macmillan, 1983.

27. CONNOR, John M. ; *The Market Power of Multinationals,* Praeger, 1977.

28. CHITALE, V.P. ; *Foreign Technology in India*, Economic and scientific Research Foundation, New Delhi, 1973.

29. CHUDSON, Welter A. ; *The International Transfer of Commercial Technology to Developing Countries*, UN Institute for Training and Research, Reports No. 13, New York, 1973.

30. COHEN, Benjamin I.; *Multinational Firms and Asian Exports,* Yale, 1975.

31. COHEN, Robert B. *et al* (ed.) ; *The Multinational Corporation A Radical Approach* (Papers by Stephen Herbert Hymer), Cambridge University Press, 1979.

32. CURZON, Gerald and CURZON, Victoria ; *The Multinational Enterprises in a Hostile World*, Macmillan, London, 1977.

33. DUNNING, John H. ; *The Multinational Enterprises— The Background*, George Allen and Unwin, London, 1971.

34. DYMSZA, William A. ; *Multinational Business Strategy*, Mc-Graw Hill, New York, 1972.

35. DGTD, India; *Handbook of Foreign Collaboration*, New Delhi, 1974.

36. DEB, Kalipada ; *Foreign Resources and Development in India*, Heritage, New Delhi, 1982.

37. EITEMAN, David K. and STONEHILL, A.I. ; *Multinational Business Finance*, Reading, Massachusettes Addison Wesley, 1973.

38. EELLS, Richard ; *Global Corporations, Systems of World Economic Power*, The Free Press, New York, 1976.

39. FATEMI, Nasrollah S. *et al* ; *MNCs —The Problems and Prospects*, A.S. Barnes & Co. New Jersey, 1976.

40. FRANK, Isaiah ; *Foreign Enterprise in Developing Countries*, Johns Hopkins University Press, 1980.

41. FRIEDMAN, W.G. and BENGUIN, J. : *Joint International Business Ventures in Developing Countries*, Columbia University Press, New York, 1971.

42. FITT, Yan *et al* ; *The World Economic Crisis*, Zed Press, Caledonian Road, London, 1976 (translated in 1980).

43. FELD, Werner J. ; *MNCs and UN Politics—the quest for Code of Conduct*, University of New Orleans, Pergamon Press, 1980.

44. FRIEVES, Forest L. ; *Transnationalism in World Politics and Business*, Pergamon Press, 1980.

45. GILPIN, Robert ; *US Power and the Multinational Corporations The Political Economy of Foreign Direct Investment*, Macmillan, 1976.

46. GIRWAN, Norman ; *Foreign Capital and Economic Development in Jamaica*, Institute of Social and Economic Research, University of West Indies, Jamaica, 1971.

47. GOODSELL, Charles T. ; *American Corporations and Peruvian Politics*, Harward University Press, 1974.

48. GUNNEMANN, John P. ; *The National State and TNCs in Conflict* (Praeger Special Studies in International Economics and Development), Praeger, London.

49. GANGULI, B.N. ; *Multinational Corporations*, S. Chand, New Delhi, 1974.

50. GREEN, James and DUERR, Michael G. ; *Inter-Company Transactions in the Multinational Firm*, National Industrial Conference Board, New York, 1969.

51. GUPTA, Bhupesh ; *The Big Loot : A brief study of Foreign Exploitation in India*, Peoples' Publishing House, New Delhi, 1962.

52. GUNTER, H. (ed.) ; *Transnational Industrial Relations : The Impact of Multinational Corporation*, Macmillan, New York, 1972.

53. GUPTA, J.N. (ed.) ; *Directory of Foreign Collaboration in India*, 3 Volumes, The Indian Overse as Publication, New Delhi, 1974.

54. GRIFFIN, Keith ; *International Inequality and National Poverty*, Macmillan, 1978.

55. GOYAL, S.K. ; *Monopoly Capital and Public Policy*, Allied Publishers, New Delhi, 1979.

56. HELLMANN, Rainer ; *Transnational Control of Multinational Corporations*, Praeger, 1977.

57. HAYS, R.D.; *International Business : An Introduction to the World of the Multinational Firms*, Prentice Hall, Englewood Cliffs, 1972.

58. HAZARI, R.K. (ed.) ; *Foreign collaboration*, University of Bombay, Bombay, 1967.

59. HODGES, Michael ; *Multinational Corporations and National Governments*, Lexington Books, Saxon House, 1974.

60. HUMBLE, John ; *The Responsible Multinational Enterprise*, Foundation for Business Responsibility, London, 1975.

61. HEENAN, David A. and PERLMUTTER Hovard V. ; *Multinational Organisation Development*, Addison Wasley Publishing Co., Reading, Massachusettes, 1979.

62. HELLOR, Tom ; *Poor Health and Rich Profits : Multinational Drug Companies in the Third World*, Spokesman Book, Bertrand Russel Peace Foundation, Nottingham, 1977.

63. HIRSCHMAN, Albert O. ; *The Passion and Interest, Political Arguments for Capitalism before its Triumph*, Princeton University Press, 1977.

64. ILO ; *The Impact of Multinational Enterprises on Employment and Training*, Geneva, 1976.

65. ——- *International Principles and Guidelines on Social Policy for Multinational Enterprises, Their Usefulness and Feasibility*, Geneva, 1976.

66. ILO ; *Multinational Enterprises and Social Policy*, Geneva, 1973.

67. INDIA, Ministry of Petroleum and Chemicals ; *Report of the Committee on Drugs and Pharmaceutical Industry*, 1975.

68. ILIOU, Ilia *et al* ; *Multinational Hypermonopolies : The Disintegration of Imperialism*, Gutenberg, 1973.

69. JOHRI, Lalit M. ; *Business Strategies of Multinational Corporations in India—Case Study of Drug and Pharmaceutical Industry*, Vision Books, 1983.

70. JHA, L.K. ; *Transnational Enterprises and Developing Countries*, Indian Investment Centre, New Delhi, 1975.

71. JORDEN, Robert S. (ed) ; *Multinational Corporations— Economic, Social and Scientific Development*, Oxford University Press, New York, 1972.

72. JACOBY, Herman N.; *Corporate Power and Social Responsibility : A Blue Print for the Future*, Macmillan, 1973.

73. JAIN, O.P. and SAVARA, S.K ; *Industrialisation and Multinationsals*, Commercial Publications, New Delhi, 1981.

74. KENNET, Wayland *et al* ; *Sovereignty and Multinational Companies*, Fabian Tract, 1971.

75. KAPOOR, A. and GRUB, Phillip D. (eds) ; *The Multinational Enterprise in Transition*, Darwin Press, 1972.

76. KAPOOR, Ashok ; *Planning for International Business Negotiations*, Cambridge, Massachusettes, 1975.

77. KINDLEBERGER, C.P. (ed.) ; *International Corporations*, Cambridge, MIT Press, 1970.

78. KACKER, Madhav ; *Marketing Adaptations of US Business Firms in India*, Sterling, New Delhi, 1974.

79. KOUL, A.K. ; *A Bonanza or an Illusion for the Developing Countries' Economies*, Bangalore Christian Institute for the Study of Religion and Society, 1976.

80. KRAUSE, Lawrence ; *The International Economic System and the Multinational Corporation*, Brooking Institution, 1971.

81. KRAGENAU, Henry ; *International Direct Investment,* 1950-73, IER.

82. KURIAN, K. Mathew ; *Impact of Foreign Capital on the Indian Economy,* Peoples' Publishing House, 1966.

83. LALL, Sanjaya ; *The Multinational Corporation,* Macmillan, 1980.

84. —— *The Indirect Employment Effects of MNEs in Developing Countries,* Oxford University Institute of Economics and Statistics Working Paper No. 3, ILO, Geneva, 1979.

85. —— and Elek, A. ; *Balance of payments and Income Effects of Private Foreign Investment in Manufacturing : Case Studies of India and Iran,* UNCTAD, Document No. TD/B/C. 3(u)/ Misc. 1 Dec. 1971.

86. —— *Less Developed Countries and Transfer Pricing by Multinational Corporations,* Monthly Review, 1974.

87. —— *Major Issues in the Transfer of Technology to Developing Countries : A Case Study of the Pharmaceutical Industry,* UNCTAD, TD/B/C. 6/4, 1975.

88. LILIENTHAL, David E. ; *The Multinational Corporations, Development and Resource Corporation,* New York, 1960.

89. LITVAK, Isaiah A. and MAULE, Christopher J. ; *Foreign Investments : The Experience of Host Countries,* Praeger, New York, 1970.

90. LEONTIFF, Wassily ; *The Future of the World Economy,* Oxford University Press, London, 1977.

91. LONG, Frank ; *Restrctive Business Practices : TNCs and Development — A Survey,* Martinus Nijhoff Publishing, Boston, 1981.

92. LOUIS, Wm. Roger (ed.) ; *Imperialism, New Viewpoints,* Franklin Watts, London, 1976

93. MYRDAL, Gunnar ; *The Political Element in the Development of Economic Theory,* 1953.

94. MANSER, W.A.P. ; *The Financial Role of Multinational Enterprises*, Cassell, Associated Business Programme, London, 1973.

95. MODELSKY, G. (ed).; *Multinational Corporations and World Order*, Beverly Hills, Sage Publications, London, 1972.

96. MORAN, Theodore H. ; *Multinational Corporations and the Politics of Dependence—Copper in Chile*, Oxford University Press, Bombay, 1974.

97. MASON, R.H. *et al* ; *The Economics of International Business*, John Wiley, New York, 1975.

98. MATHEW, Harry G. ; *Multinational Corporations and the Black Power*, 1976.

99. MAXWELL, Stephen ; *Scotland Multinationals and the Third World*, Mainstream Publishing, Edinburgh, 1982.

100. McMILLAN, C. Gonzales *et al* ; *International Enterprise in a Developing Economy*, Michigan State University Press, 1964.

101. MICHE, Joachim ; *Multinationals in the North South Conflict*, Zurich, Verlag, Ex Libri, Weinheim, 1976.

102. MIKADASHI, Zuhayr ; *The International Politics of Natural Resources*, Cornell University Press, 1976.

103. MAGADOFF, Harry ; *The Age of Imperialism* : *The Economics of US Foreign Policy*, Monthly Review Press, New York, 1969.

104. McHALE, V.E. *et al* (ed.) ; *Evaluating Transnational Programmes in Government and Business*, Pergamon Press, 1980.

105. MARX, Karl, *Das Kapital*, Progress Publishers, Moscow.

106. MATTEHAT, Armond ; *Multinational Corporations and Control of Culture*, Harvestor Press.

107. NEGANDHI, A.R. and PRASAD, S. Benjamin ; *The Frightening Angles* : *A Study of US Multinationals in Developing Countries*, The Kent University Press, Kent, 1975.

108. NEGANDHI. A.R. (ed.) : *Functioning of the Multinational Corporations—A Global Comparative Study*, Pergamon Press, 1980.

109. OECD ; *International Investment and Multinational Enterprises*, Paris, 1976.

110. —— ; *Choice and Adaptation of Technology in Developing Countries*, Review of Discussion held at the Study Session organise by the OECD Development Centre, Paris, 7-9 Nov. 1972.

111. OH, Moonsong ; *The Role of Multinational Corporations in the Transfer of Technology to the Developing Countries*, Ann Arbor, Michigan University of Microfilms, 1970.

112. P.S. PRUTHI, Surinder ; *Multinationals in Developing Countries*, Leslie Sawhny Programme of Training for Democracy, Friederich, Vaumann, Stiftung, 1975.

113. PATHAK, Arvind V. ; *Managing Multinational Corporations*, Praeger, New York, 1974.

114. PARKER, J.E.S. ; *The Economies of Innovation : The National and Multinational Enterprise in Technological Change*, Longman, London, 1974.

115. PRAKASH, OM ; *Economic Sins of Nations*, Progressive Publishers, Calcutta, 1978.

116. PAQUET, G. (ed.) ; *The Multinational Firm and Nation State*, Collier-Macmillan, 1972.

117. PENROSE, Edith T. ; *The Large International Firm in Developing Countries : The International Petroleum Industry*, George Allen and Unwin Ltd., 1968.

118. RADICE, Hugo (ed.) ; *International Firms* : Modern Imperialism, Penguin Books, 1975.

119. ROBOCK, Stefan H. and SIMMONDS, Kenneth ; *International Business and Multinational Enterprise*, Richard P. Irving Inc. Homewood Illinois, 1973.

120. ROLFE, Sidney E. and DAMN, Walter (eds.) ; *The Multinational Corporations in the World Economy*, Praeger, New York, 1970.

121. RAMU, S. Shiva ; *Multinational Firms, Strategies and Environment*, Sultan Chand & Sons, Delhi.

122. R.B.I. ; *Foreign Collaboration in Indian Industry*, 1st Survey Report, Bombay, 1968.

123. R.B.I. ;   — —,   2nd Survey Report, Bombay, 1974.

124. SKINNER, Wikham ; *American Industries in Developing Economies*, Wiley, 1968.

125. SRIVASTAVA, P.K. ; *Foreign Collaboration, its Significance in India's Industrial Progress*, Shiv Lal Agrawal & Co., Agra, 1975.

126. SIDHARTHA, N.S. ; *Conglomerates and Multinationals in India*, Allied Publishers, New Delhi, 1981.

127. SOLOMAN, Lewis D. ; *MNCs and the Emerging World Order*, Kennikat Press, New York, 1978.

128. SUBRAHMANIAN, K.K. ; *Impact of Capital and Technology —A Study of Foreign Collaborations in Indian Industry*, Peoples' Publishing House, New Delhi, 1972.

129. SUBRAHMANIAN, K.K. and PILLAI, P. Mohan ; *Multi-nationals and Indian Exports*, Allied Publishers, New Delhi, 1979.

130. SAMPSON, Anthony ; *The Sovereign State : The Secret History of ITT*, Hodder and Stoughton, 1973.

131. STREETEN, P.P. and LALL, Sanjaya ; *Main Findings of a Study of Private Foreign Investment in Selected Developing Countries*, UNCTAD, TD/B/C.3/111.

132. STEINER, G.A. and CANNON, W.M. ; *Multinational Corporate Planning*, Macmillan, New York, 1966.

133. SAID, Abdul Aziz and SIMMONS, Luiz R. ; *The New Sovereigns : Multinational Corporations an as World Powers*, Prentice Hall, 1975.

134. SANGAL, P.S. ; *Multinational and their Impact on India*, Christian Institute for the Study of Religion and Society, Bangalore, 1976.

135. SANGAL P.S. ; *National and Multinational Companies, Some Legal Issues*, Bhagwati International Enterprise, New Delhi, 1981.

136. SALERA, Virgil ; *Multinational Business*, Mifflin Company, Houghton, Boston, 1969.

137. SETHI, S. Prakash ; *Advanced Cases in Multinational Business Operations*, Palisades, Goodyear Publishing Co., 1972.

138. —— ; *Up against the Corporate Wall—Modern Corporations and Social Issues of the Seventies*, Third ed. Prentice Hall, Inc., Englewood Cliffs, New Jersey, 1977.

139. SHOJI, Shiba ; *A Cross National Comparison of Labour Management with reference to Technology Transfer*, Institute of Developing Economies, (Occasional Papers Series No. 11), Tokyo, 1973.

140. SARKAR, Nihar K.G. (ed.) ; *Foreign Investment and Economic Development in Asia*, Orient Longman, Bombay, 1976.

141. STEPHEN, Hugh ; *The Coming Clash : The Impact of Multinational Corporation on National Interests*, Saturday Review, 1972.

142. SILVERMAN, Milton and LEE, Philip R. ; *Pills, Profits and Politics*, University of California Press Berkley, Los Angeles, 1974.

143. SINGH, V.B.; *Multinational Corporations and India*, Sterling, New Delhi, 1979.

144. SWAMI, Dalip S.; *Multinational Corporations and the Third World Economy*, Alps (International) Publishers, New Delhi, 1980.

145. TUGENDHAT, C. ; *The Multinationals*, Middlesex, Penguin, 1973.

146. TURNER, Louis ; *Invisible Empires : Multinational Companies and the Modern World*, Hamish Hamilton, London, 1970.

147. TSURUMI, Yoshi ; *Multinational Management : Business Strategy and Government Policy*, Ballinger Publishing Co., Cambridge, Massachusettes, 1977.

148. TINDALL, Robert E. ; *Multinational Enterprises*, Oceania Publications, Inc., Dobbs Fery, Sijthoff, Leiden, 1975.

149. US Congress Senate Committee on Foreign Relations ; *Multinational Corporations and US Foreign Policy* : Hearing before the Sub-Committee on Multinational Corporations, Part 2, Washington D.C., 1973, pp. 517-1092.

150. US Bureau of International Commerce ; *The Multinational Corporations* : *Studies on US Foreign Investment*, Vol. 2, Washington DC, 1972.

151. VAITSOS, Constantine V. ; *Inter-Country Income Distribution and Transnational Enterprises*, Clarendon Press, Oxford, 1974.

152. VERNON, R. ; *The Economic and Political Consequences of Multinational Enterprises—An Anthology*, Harward Boston, 1972.

153. VERNON, R. ; *Sovereignty at Bay* : *The Multinational Spread of US Enterprises*, Basic Books, New York, 1971.

154. —— ; *Storm over the Multinationals*, The Real Issues, Macmillan Press, 1977.

155. —— ; *Restrictive Business Practices, The Operation of Multinational US Enterprise in Developing Countries* : *Their Role in Trade and Development*, UN Publications, Sales No. E. 72. II D. 16.

156. WILEZYNSKI, J. ; *The Multinationals and East West Relations* : *Towards Transideological Collaboration*, Macmillan, London, 1976.

157. WILKINS, Mira ; *The Emergence of Multinational Enterprises* (American Business Abroad from Colonial Era to 1914), Harward University Press, Cambridge, 1970.

158. WILKINS, Mira ; *The Maturing Multinational Enterprises* : *American Business Abroad from 1914 to 1970*, Harward University Press, Cambridge, 1970.

159. WATT, George C. *et al* ; *Accounting For Multinational Corporations*, Dow Jones Irvin Homewood, Illinois, 1977.

160. *World Development Report*, 1984.

161. *World Economic Outlook*, 1984.

ARTICLES

1. ABDEL-Malek, Talaat ; *"Foreign Ownership and Export Performance,"* Journal of International Business Studies, Vol. 5, No. 2, Fall pp. 1-14.

2. ABELL, Peter ; *"Parent Companies' Control of Subsidiaries —Evidence from the UK,"* Multinational Business, No. 1, pp. 11-22.

3. ADAM, Gyorgy, *World Corporations : Dual Power in the International Economy*, The New Hungarian Quarterly, Vol. 7, Nos. 3-4, pp. 349-367.

4. AGGARWAL, Raj ; *Multinational Companies and Economic Development : Prospects for Developing Countries*, Conference Paper, IIT, New Delhi (Jan. 6) 1976.

5. AHARONI, Yair ; *The Definition of a Multinational Corporation*, Quarterly Review of Economics and Business, Vol. 11, No. 3, Autumn, pp. 27-38, 1971.

6. ALGER, C. F.; *The Multinational Corporation and the Future International System*, The Annals of the American Academy of Social Science, Vol. 403, September 1972.

7. ASH, Roy L. ; *New Anatomy of World Business*, Columbia Journal of World Business, Vol. 5, No. 2, March 1970, pp. 90-3.

8. BALL, George W. ; *Multinational Corporations and Nation States*, Atlantic Community Quarterly, Vol. 5, Summer, pp. 247-253.

9. BARANSON, J. ; *Transfer of Technical Knowledge by International Corporations to Developing Economies*, American Economic Review, Paper and Proceedings, Vol. 56, May, pp. 259-67, 1966.

10. BARANSON, J; *Technology Transfer Through the International Firm*, American Economic Review, Papers and Proceedings, Vol. 60, May 1970, pp. 435-40 and 449-53.

11. BAUM, Daniel J. ; *Global Corporation* : *An American Challenge to the Nation-state*, Iowa Law Review, 55 pp. 410-437, 1969-70.

12. BEHRMAN, Jack N. : *Foreign Investment Muddle*, Columbia Journal of World Business, Fall, pp. 51-60, 1965.

13. BEHRMAN, Jack N. ; *Multinational Corporations and National Sovereignty*, Columbia Journal of World Business, March-April, pp. 15-22, 1969.

14. BEHRMAN Jack N. ; *Multinational Corporations, Transnational Interests and National Sovereignty*, Columbia Journal of World Business, Vol. 4, March 1969, pp. 15-21.

15. BEHRMAN, Jack N. ; *Can Government Slay the dragon of Multinational Enterprise*? European Business, No. 28, Winter, pp. 53-64, 1971.

16. —— ; *The Multinational Enterprise* : *The Initiatives and Governmental Reactions*, The Journal of International Law and Economics, pp. 215-233, Jan. 1972.

17. —— ; *Actors and Factors in Policy Decisions on Foreign Direct Investment*, World Development, pp. 1-14, Aug., 1974.

18. BENOIT, E. ; *Attack on the Multinationals*, Columbia Journal of World Business, Vol. 7, Nov. 1972, pp. 15-22.

19. BERGSTEN, C. Fred ; *The Threat to the Third World*, Foreign Policy, Summer, 1973.

20. BHATT, R.S. ; *Foreign Collaboration and Joint Ventures*, Journal of Industry and Trade, Vol. 23, No. 10, 1973, pp. 73-81.

21. BODDEWYN, J.J. and CRACCO, F.F. ; *The Political Game in International Business*, Columbia Journal of World Business, Vol. 7, Jan-Feb. 1972, pp. 45-56.

22. CATERORA, Philip R. ; *Multinational Enterprise and Nationalism*, MSU Business Topics, Vol. 19, Spring 1971, pp. 49-56.

23. DEO, Som ; *The Multinational Corporations and the Developing Economies*, Economic Affairs, Vol. 20, No. 8, Aug., 1975.

24. —— ; *Multinational Corporation—The Exploiting Feuds*, Economic Affairs, Vol. 25, Nos. 1-3, 4-6, and 7-9, Jan-March, April-June and July-Aug 1980.

25. DRUCKER, Peter F. ; *Multinationals and Developing Countries : Myths and Realities*, Foreign Affairs, Vol. 53, Oct. 1974.

26. DUNN, M.R. ; *The Impact of the Multinationals*, Journal of the Institute of Bankers, Vol. 95, pt. 5, Oct. 1974.

27. DUNNING, John H. ; *Multinational Enterprises and Trade Flows in Less Developed Countries*, University of Reading, Discussion Papers in International Investment and Business Studies, No. 1, Feb. 1973.

28. DUREN, Albrecht ; *Multinational Companies as a Political Problem*, World Today, Vol. 28, No. 11, Nov. 1972, pp. 437-482.

29. EVANS, Peter B. ; *National Autonomy and Economic Development Critical Perspective on MNCs in Poor Countries*, International Organisation, Vol. 25, Summer, 1971 pp. 675-92.

30. GALLOWAY, J.F. ; *The Military Industrial Linkages of US Based Multinational Corporations*, International Studies Quarterly, December 1972. pp. 491-510.

31. GOYAL, S.K. ; *Some Aspects of the Operations of Multinational Corporations in India*, Social Action, Vol. 30. No. 4, Oct-Dec 1980, pp. 367-377.

32. HELLEINER, G.K. ; *Manufactured Exports from Less Developed Countries and Multinational Firms*, Economic Journal, Vol. 83, No. 329, March 1973, pp. 21-49.

33. HIRSCH, Seev ; *The Extent and Form of the Firm's International Involvement*, Israel Institute of Business Research, Tel Aviv, University Working Paper, 44/74, 1974.

34. HIRSCHMAN, Albert O.; *The Political Economy of Import— Substituting Industrialisation in Latin America*, The Quarterly Journal of Economics, 82, Feb. 1968, pp. 1-32.

35. HOGAN, W.P. ; *Multinational Firms, Labour Mitigation and Trade Flows*, Journal of Industrial Relations, Vol. 14, Sept. 1972, pp. 225-237.

36. HORST, T. ; *National Control of International Firms*, Harward University Institute of Economic Research, Discussion Papers No. 94, December 1969.

37. —— ; *Theory of Multinational Firm* : *Optimal Behaviour under Different Tariff and Tax Rates*, Journal of Political Economy, Vol. 79, Sept. 1979, pp. 1059-72.

38. HOSKINS, W.R. ; *LDCs and the MNCs* : *Will they Develop together*, Columbia Journal of World Business, Vol. 6, No. 5, Sept-Oct. 1971, pp. 61-70.

39. HOWARD, C.G. ; *The Extent of Nativisation of Management in Overseas Affiliates of Multinational Firms* : A World Wide Study, Indian Management, Vol. 10, Jan. 1971, pp. 11-20.

40. HYMER, Stephen ; *The Efficiency (Contradictions) of Multinational Corporations*, American Economic Review, Vol. 60, No. 2, May 1970, pp. 441-448.

41. —— ; *Partners in Development* : *The Multinational Corporation and its allies*, New Statesman, No. 1, 1970, pp. 4-14.

42. JOHNSON, R. ; *The Multinational Corporation and the Nation State*, Melbourne University Law Review, Vol. 9, No. 3, June 1974, pp. 513-527.

43. KAISER, Karl ; *Transnational Politics* : *Toward a Theory of Multinational Politics*, International Organisation, Vol. 25, Autumn 1971, pp. 790-817.

44. KAPOOR, Ashok ; *Foreign Collaborations in India*, The Trademark and Copyright Journal of Research and Education, Summer, 1966, pp. 213-58 ; Fall, pp. 349-87.

45. KNOPPERS, Antonie T. ; *The Multinational Corporation in the Third World*, Columbia Journal of World Business, Vol. 5, No. 4, July-Aug. 1970, pp. 33-39.

46. KORTH, Christopher M. ; *A Devaluation Dichotomy* : *Headquarters V/s Subsidiary*, M.S.U. Business Topics, Autumn, 1972.

47. LALL, Sanjay : *Transfer pricing by Multinational Manufacturing Firms*, Oxford Bulletin of Economics and Statistics, Vol. 35, Aug, 1973, pp. 173-195.

48. —— ; *The International Pharmaceutical Industry and Less Developed Countries, with special reference to India*, Oxford Bulletin of Economics and Statistics, Vol. 36, August 1974, pp. 143-172.

49. —— ; *Multinationals and Development* : *A New Look*, National Westminster Bank Review, Feb. 1975.

50. —— ; *The Patent System of the Transfer of Technology to Less Developed Countries*, Journal of World Trade Law, Vol. 10, No 1, Jan-Feb.1976, pp. 1-16.

51. LEFF, Nathaniel H.; *Multinational Corporate Pricing Strategy in the Developing Countries*, Journal of International Business Studies, Vol. 6, No. 2, Fall, 1975, p. 55.

52. MASON, R. Hal and MASSON, Francis G. ; *Balance of Payments Costs and Conditions of Technology Transfers to Latin America*, Journal of International Business Studies, Vol. 5, No. 1 Spring, 1974, pp. 73-89.

53. MASON, R. Hal ; *The Conflicts Between Host Countries and the Multinational Enterprise*, California Management Review, Vol. 17, Autumn 1974, pp. 5-14.

54. MULLER, Ronald E. ; *National Instability and Global Corporations* : *Must They Grow Together* ? Business and Society Review, No. 11, Autumn, 1974, pp. 61-72.

55. MULLER, Ronald E. and MORGENSTERN, R.D.; *Multinational Corporations and Balance of Payments Impact in LDCs : An Econometric Analysis of Export Pricing Behaviour*, Kyklos, No. 2, 1974, pp. 304-21.

56. MASCARANHAS, O.A. ; *Multinational Impact as a Function of Host Government Pressure, Social Action*, Vol. 30, No. 4, Oct-Dec 1980, pp. 378-402.

57. NEGANDHI, Anant R. ; *Multinational Corporations and Host Governments*, News India, June 1975.

58. NYE, Joseph S. ; *Multinational Corporations in World Politics*, Foreign Affairs, Vol. 53, No. 1, October 1974.

59. PENROSE, Edith T. ; *Problems Associated with the Growth of International Firms*, The Rhodesian Journal of Economics, Vol. 3, Dec. 1969, pp. 1-7.

60. —— ; *The State and Multinational Enterprise in Less Developed Countries*, in Dunning, John H. (ed,) The Multinational Enterprise, George Allen & Unwin Ltd., 1971, pp. 221-39.

61. —— ; *International Patenting and Less Developed Countries*, The Economic Journal, Vol. 83, No. 2, Sept. 1973, pp. 768-785.

62. PERLMUTTER, Howard, V. ; *The Tortious Evolution of the Multinational Corporation*, Columbia Journal of World Business Vol. 4, No. 2, Jan./Feb. 1969, pp. 9-18.

63. PERLMUTTER, *Geocentric Giants to Rule World Business*, Business Abroad, Vol. 94, April 1969.

64. PLASSCHAERT, Sylvain ; *Multinational Enterprises, Exchange Markets and Monetary Crises*, Centre for managerial Economics and Econometrics, University of Antwerp, Working Paper, 76-19, Jan. 1976.

65. RUBIN, Seymour J. ; *Multinational Enterprise and National Sovereignty : A Sceptic Analysis*, Law and Policy in International Business, Vol. 3, 1971, pp. 1-4.

66. SACHDEV, J.C. ; *Disinvestment : A New Challenge to Multinationals and a New Threat to Developing Countries*, Multinational Business, No. 3, 1974, p. 28.

67. VAITSOS, C.V. ; *Patents Revisited : Their Function in Developing Countries*, Journal of Development Studies, Oct. 1972, pp. 71-97.

68. VAITSOS, C.V. ; *Strategic Choices in the Commercialisation of Technology : The point of view of Developing Countries*, International Social Science Journal, 25 (3) 1973, pp. 370-86.

69. VENU, S. ; *The Multinationals and Developing Societies : A profile of the Future*, Futures, Vol. 6, No. 2, April 1974, pp. 133-141.

70. VERNON, Reymond ; *Multinational Enterprise and National Sovereignty*, Harward Business Review, Vol. 45, No. 2, 1967.

71. VERNON, Reymond ; *The Multinational Enterprise : Power V/S Sovereignty*, Foreign Affairs, Vol. 49, No. 4, July 1971, pp. 736-51.

UN PUBLICATIONS

1. *Transnational Corporations in World Development : A Reexamination*, UN Doc. E/C. 10/38 of March 10, 1978.

2. *National Legislations and Regulations relating to the Transnational Corporations*, Doc. ST/CTC/6.

3. *The Impact of the Multinational Corporations on Development and International Relations*, UN Doc. E/5500/Rev. 1 : ST/ESA/6,

4. UNCTAD : *Restrictive Business Practices : The Operation of Multinational Enterprises in Developing Countries, Their Role in Trade and Development*, 1972.

5. *The Role of Patents in Transfer of Technology to Developing Countries*, New York, 1964.

6. UNCTAD, *The Channels of Mechanism of Transfer of Technology from Developed to Developing Countries*, TD/B/AC. 11.5.

7. UNCTAD, *The Role of Transnational Corporations in the Trade in the Manufacturers and Semi-manufactures of Developing Countries*, Geneva, 1975.

8. ILO, Geneva, *MNE and Social Policy*, 1973.

9. *The Impact of Multinational Corporations on International Relations*, Technical Papers : Taxation, Sales No. E. 74. II. A. 6.

10. *The Acquisition of Technology from Multinational Corporations by Developing Countries*, Sales No. E. 74. II. A. 7.

11. *Transnational Corporations : Issues involved in Formulation of a Code of Conduct*, Reprint of Document with Symbol E/C. 10/17, Sales No. E. 77. II. A. 5.

12. *Survey of Research on Transnational Corporations*, Sales No. E. 77. II. A. 16.

13. *National Legislation and Regulations relating to Transnational Corporations*, Sales No. E. 78. II. A. 3.

14. *Supplement to National Legislation and Regulations relating to Transnational Corporations*, Sales No. E. 80. II. A. 5.

15. *Transnational Corporations : Activities of Transnational Corporations in Southern Africa : Impact of Financial and Social Structure*, Sales No. E. 78. II. A. 6.

16. *Transnational Corporations in the Pharmaceutical Industry*, Sales No. E. 79. II. A. 3.

17. *Measures strengthening the Negotiation Capacity of Governments in their relations with Transnational Corporations : Technology Transfer Through Transnational Corporations*, Sales No. E. 79. II. A. 6.

18. *Transnational Corporation Linkages in Developing Countries. The case of backward Linkages via sub-contracting*, Sales No. E. 81 II. A. 4.

19. *The CTC Reports*, Vol. 1, No. 1 to Vol. 1, No. 10.

20. *Transnational Corporations : A Select Bibliography*, Dag Hammerskjold Library, New York, 1975.

21. *Foreign Investment in Developing Countries,* E/4446/Corr. 1 Sales No. E. 68. II. D. 2.

22. *Summary of the Hearings before the Group of Eminent Persons to study the Impact of Multinational Corporations on Development and on International Relations,* IX, New York, 1974.

LIST OF JOURNALS

1. American Economic Review, Nashville, Tennessee, USA.
2. Company News and Notes, New Delhi.
3. Canadian Journal of Economics, Toronto, Canada.
4. Columbia Journal of World Business, New York.
5. Economic Journal, Cambridge, England.
6. Foreign Affairs, New York, USA.
7. Foreign Trade Review, New Delhi.
8. Financial Express, New Delhi.
9. Indian Management, New Delhi.
10. Journal of Development Studies, England.
11. Journal of Political Economy, Illinois, USA.
12. Journal of International Economics.
13. Journal of International Business Studies, New Jersey, USA.
14. Journal of International Law and Economics, Washington, USA.
15. Kyklos.
16. MSU Business Topics, Michigan, USA.
17. Multinational Business, England.
18. Oxford Bulletin of Economics and Statistics.
19. Social Action, New Delhi.
20. Third World Quarterly.
21. The Economic Times, Bombay.

Index

223